MEASURING UP
TO THE
BALDRIGE

MEASURING UP

TO THE

BALDRIGE

A
QUICK & EASY
SELF-ASSESSMENT
GUIDE FOR
ORGANIZATIONS OF
ALL SIZES

DONALD C. FISHER

amacom

American Management Association

New York • Atlanta • Boston • Chicago • Kansas City • San Francisco • Washington D.C.
Brussels • Mexico City • Tokyo • Toronto

Library of Congress Cataloging-in-Publication Data

Fisher, Donald C.
    Measuring up to the Baldrige : a quick & easy self-assessment
guide for organizations of all sizes / Donald C. Fisher.
        p. cm.
    Includes bibliographical references.
    ISBN 0-8144-0256-9
    1. Malcolm Baldrige National Quality Award. 2. Total quality
management—Awards—United States. I. Title.
HD62. 15.F56 1994
658.5'62' 07973--dc20   94-22220
                                                            CIP

Printing number

10 9 8 7 6 5 4 3 2 1

To my father,
Alvin G. Fisher,
who was my standard of excellence
during childhood and as an adult,
with love and appreciation

Contents

Foreword

Many American companies and some foreign companies have been using the Malcolm Baldrige criteria for internal assessments to determine the completeness of their quality systems. In addition, this same criteria is used for most state quality award assessments as well as for the National Malcolm Baldrige Quality Award. During a recent visit of twenty-one industrial executives from India to our company, they indicated they had compared the Deming Award criteria, the European Quality Award criteria, the Baldrige criteria, and ISO-9000 criteria, and decided to use the Baldrige criteria to evaluate their quality systems.

Based on our experience, the Baldrige criteria is in such detail that it requires considerable training to be useful to line managers in organizational assessments. This assessment manual will be a great tool in assisting staff and line managers to self-assess the organization with enough standardization to give consistent scoring. The results will be a list of strengths and opportunities for continuous improvement, which will make your organization better.

Dr. Fisher writes from a background of experience as a manager, educator, Baldrige examiner, and consultant. He knows the type of problems users encounter because of this experience, and this makes this book very practical. I have worked with Dr. Fisher on the Tennessee Quality Award Board of Directors, and find him very knowledgeable, helpful, and energetic. I would expect diligent use of this manual would generate many opportunities for continuous improvements and increased customer satisfaction.

Bill Garwood
President, Tennessee Eastman Division
Eastman Chemical Company
Winner of the 1994 Malcolm Baldrige National Quality Award

Preface

This manual is designed to help employees and employee teams conduct a comprehensive assessment of their organization. Based on the Malcolm Baldrige National Quality Award criteria, the manual contains ninety-one areas in which employees can assess both short- and long-term strategic improvements and develop or enhance their organization's existing business planning process.

A practical breakdown of the Baldrige questions will prove useful in writing an application for any corporate, city, state, or national quality award that is based on Baldrige criteria. In addition, this assessment manual is an excellent tool for encouraging total employee involvement in the organization's strategic planning process.

Since 1987, the Baldrige criteria have received enormous criticism for being too complex to use as a template for continuous improvement, especially for individuals who have little or no experience in using the criteria. I have taken the liberty of rewording them. Because the Baldrige criteria use complicated, compounded questions and explanation notes that are difficult to understand, I also recommend that several employees located at various levels throughout the organization conduct the assessment. This will allow many sets of eyes to bring clarity and input into the assessment process. This manual therefore provides:

- A quality check for an organization's continuous improvement efforts regarding total integration of quality and business plan initiatives
- A simplified understanding of the Baldrige questions
- User-friendly guidelines for organizational self-assessment and strategic planning
- A translation of complex Baldrige criteria into layman's language
- A comparison section for areas assessed, to describe both an organization with an ineffective quality management program,

referred to in this book as zero-based, and one that produces excellent results in main areas with a sound quality management program, referred to as world-class; this allows an organization to gauge where it fits between the two

- Baseline data for an organization's quality initiatives and assessment of how totally integrated its quality initiatives are
- Documentation for an organization of its areas of strength and areas needing improvement
- A means for employee teams to score their organization in seven categories, twenty-eight items, and ninety-one areas based on the Baldrige scoring process
- An annual scorebook for continuous quality improvement (maximum score 1,000 points)
- The beginnings of short-term and long-term strategic self-assessment within an organization
- A section, for each area assessed, to break down short-term and long-term strategies
- Scoring profiles for each of the seven Baldrige categories
- A quick-reference Baldrige assessment glossary
- Projection of organization priorities using the Baldrige readiness assessment bar graph
- A detailed checklist for employees who are writing a quality-award application

PART I
THE BALDRIGE

One

Introduction

I hope this manual will become an invaluable tool to

- Better understanding the Baldrige criteria
- Encouraging all levels of employees to assess or inventory their work areas and their organization as a whole
- Providing an organizational climate check based on the National Quality Award criteria
- Assessing organizational readiness to ultimately write a quality-award application for a corporate, community, state, or national quality award.

The Award criteria are directed toward delivering improved value to customers while simultaneously maximizing the overall effectiveness and productivity of the organization. They are built around seven major examination categories:

Examination Categories [1]

1. *Leadership.* The senior executives' success in creating and sustaining a culture of quality.
2. *Information and analysis.* The effectiveness of information collection and analysis for quality improvement and planning.
3. *Strategic quality planning.* The effectiveness of systems and processes for ensuring the quality of products and services.
4. *Human resource development and management.* The success of efforts to realize the full potential of the workforce to meet an organization's quality and performance objectives.
5. *Management of process quality.* The effectiveness of systems and processes for assuring the quality of products and services.
6. *Quality and operational results.* The improvement of quality and operational performance, demonstrated through qualitative measures.
7. *Customer focus and satisfaction.* The effectiveness of systems to determine customer requirements and demonstrated success in meeting them.

---

1. *Source*: NIST, *1994 Award Criteria Booklet* (Gaithersburg, Md., National Institute of Standards and Technology).

Is Anybody Still Doing the Baldrige?

To the question, "Is anybody still doing the Baldrige?" Ann T. Rothgeb, an information specialist for the Malcolm Baldrige National Quality Award office in Gaithersburg, Maryland, responded that the Baldrige Award process is "alive and well." She noted the following:

- Eighteen states currently have quality awards in place based on Baldrige criteria.
- Fourteen state awards using Baldrige criteria are under development.
- Seven major cities have Baldrige-based awards.
- Four states have senate/productivity awards incorporating Baldrige criteria.
- Twenty foreign countries have based their international awards on the Baldrige.
- The President's Quality Award Program for governmental and not-for-profit organizations is based on Baldrige criteria.
- The U.S. Air Force has based all of its continuous-improvement initiatives on the Baldrige.
- Several industries, such as the construction and software industries, base their award processes on the Baldrige.
- Education and health care are presently exploring the possibility of developing awards based on Baldrige criteria.
- Over 900,000 Baldrige criteria applications have been distributed since 1988.

It is apparent that the Baldrige Award criteria are having an impact not only on American organizations, but on international ones as well.

Business Achievement of Baldrige Award Winners

Baldrige winners have enjoyed impressive results from their investment in quality. Some examples cited by the Baldrige office include: [2]

THE RITZ-CARLTON HOTEL COMPANY has been honored by the travel industry with 121 quality awards since 1991.

GRANITE ROCK'S customer accounts have increased 38 percent from 1989 through mid-1993, while overall construction spending in its market area declined over 40 percent.

TEXAS INSTRUMENTS' DEFENSE SYSTEMS AND ELECTRONICS GROUP had a 21 percent reduction in production cycle time in 1992, with a 56 percent reduction in stock-to-production time.

---

2. *Source*: 1994 Baldrige brochure *Quality Pays–Business Achievements of Award Winners*, Malcolm Baldrige National Quality Award.

At FEDERAL EXPRESS, staff Quality Action Teams (QATs) have generated significant savings: $27 million in the personnel division since 1986, $1.5 million in revenue recovered by a computer automation QAT, and $462,000 in overtime payments saved in six months by a payroll QAT.

SOLECTRON, by focusing on customer satisfaction, has seen average yearly revenue growth of 46.8 percent, and by focusing on process quality has seen average yearly net income growth of 57.3 percent since 1989.

MOTOROLA's employee productivity has improved 100 percent since 1988 (an annual compounded rate of 12.2 percent) through robust design, continuous improvement in defect reduction, and employee education and empowerment.

The WESTINGHOUSE COMMERCIAL NUCLEAR FUEL DIVISION's product reliability has continuously improved since 1984, resulting in the industry's best fuel performance and a doubling of orders compared to 1986.

ZYTEC's internal manufacturing process yields have improved five-fold from 1988 to 1992, with customer out-of-box quality up from 99 percent to 99.8 percent and 1989 to 1992 on-time delivery improved from 75 percent to 98 percent.

WALLACE COMPANY increased sales per associate from $180,000 in 1986 to $294,000 in 1991.

The AT&T UNIVERSAL CARD program opened its one-millionth account just seventy-eight days after program launch, and a month later it was one of the top ten credit card programs in the nation.

Nuts and Bolts of the Award

As America confronts the realities of the changing global marketplace, the importance of quality to our competitiveness, productivity, and standard of living has become clear. Stemming from this renewed national awareness, the Malcolm Baldrige National Quality Improvement Act of 1987 (Pub. L. 100-107) was signed by President Ronald Reagan on August 20, 1987. The Act established the Malcolm Baldrige National Quality Award, named in honor of the former Secretary of Commerce.[3]

The purposes of this Award program are to:

- Promote quality awareness and practices in U.S. business.
- Recognize quality achievements of U.S. companies.
- Publicize successful quality strategies and programs.

---

3. *Source*: *Baldrige 1992 Handbook for the Board of Examiners*, Malcolm Baldrige National Quality Award.

The Baldrige Award program establishes guidelines and criteria that can be used by organizations in evaluating their own quality improvement efforts. It also provides guidance to American companies by disseminating information detailing how superior organizations were able to change their cultures and achieve eminence. The concept of quality improvement is directly applicable to both small and large manufacturing and service companies. The Baldrige Award encourages quality improvement throughout all sectors of the economy.

Under the Act, the secretary of commerce and the National Institute of Standards and Technology (NIST) are given responsibilities to develop and manage the Award with cooperation and financial support from the private sector. Currently, NIST is working with the American Society for Quality Control (ASQC) in Milwaukee to administer the Award.

Core Values and Concepts

The Award's core values and concepts, which run through all ninety-one areas in the criteria, are:

- Customer-driven quality
- Leadership
- Long-range outlook
- Continuous improvement
- Employee participation and development

- Design quality and prevention
- Management by fact
- Partnership development
- Corporate responsibility and citizenship
- Fast response

The Award

The awards are traditionally presented by the president of the United States and the secretary of commerce at special ceremonies in Washington, D.C. Made annually, they recognize U.S. companies that excel in quality management and quality achievement. As many as two awards may be given in each of three eligibility categories:

1. Manufacturing companies
2. Service companies
3. Small businesses

Recipients are expected to share information about their successful quality strategies with other U.S. organizations.

Basic Eligibility

The 1987 Act establishes the three eligibility categories of the Award: manufacturing, service, and small business. For-profit businesses located in the

United States or its territories may apply for the Award, whether publicly or privately owned, domestic or foreign-owned, joint ventures, incorporated firms, sole proprietorships, partnerships, or holding companies. Not eligible are local, state, and national government agencies; not-for-profit organizations; trade associations; and professional societies. But these organizations may use the Award criteria in their quest for continuous self-improvement.

Additional information on eligibility is presented in the *1994 Award Criteria.*

Organization of the Award Program

Building active partnerships in the private sector, and between the private sector and government, is fundamental to the success of the Award in improving quality in the United States.

Support by the private sector for the Award program in the form of funds, volunteer effort, and participation in information transfer is strong and growing rapidly.

The Foundation for the Malcolm Baldrige National Quality Award

The Foundation for the Malcolm Baldrige National Quality Award was created to foster the success of the program. The foundation's main objective is to raise funds to permanently endow the Award program.

Prominent leaders from U.S. companies serve as foundation trustees to ensure that the foundation's objectives are accomplished. Donor organizations vary in size and type and are representative of many kinds of businesses and business groups.

NIST

Responsibility for the Award is assigned to the Department of Commerce. NIST, an agency of the department's Technology Administration, manages the Award program.

NIST's goals are to aid U.S. industry through research and services; to contribute to public health, safety, and the environment; and to support the U.S. scientific and engineering research communities. NIST conducts basic and applied research in the physical sciences and engineering, and it develops measurement techniques, test methods, and standards. Much of NIST's work relates directly to quality and to quality-related requirements in technology development and technology utilization.

ASQC

ASQC assists in administering the Award program under contract to NIST. ASQC is dedicated to the advancement of the theory and

Figure 1.   Award winners from 1988 to 1993.

Manufacturing	Service	Small Business

1993 Award Winners

Eastman Chemical
  Company
Kingsport, Tenn.

Ames Rubber
  Corporation
Hamburg, N.J.

1992 Award Winners

AT&T Network Systems
  Group
Transmission Systems
Business Unit
Morristown, N.J.

AT&T Universal Card
  Services
Jacksonville, Fla.

Granite Rock Company
Watsonville, Calif.

Texas Instruments, Inc.
Defense Systems &
  Electronics Group
Dallas, Tex.

The Ritz-Carlton Hotel
  Company
Atlanta, Ga.

1991 Award Winners

Solectron Corporation
San Jose, Calif.

Marlow Industries
Dallas, Tex.

Zytec Corporation
Eden Prairie, Minn.

1990 Award Winners

Cadillac Motor Car
  Company
San Jose, Calif.

Federal Express
  Corporation
Memphis, Tenn.

Wallace Company, Inc.
Houston, Tex.

IBM Rochester
Rochester, Minn.

1989 Award Winners

Milliken & Company
Spartanburg, S.C.

Xerox Business Products
and Systems
Stamford, Conn.

1988 Award Winners

Motorola, Inc.
Schaumburg, Ill.

Globe Metallurgical, Inc.
Cleveland, Ohio

Westinghouse Commercial
  Nuclear Fuel Division
Pittsburgh, Pa.

practice of quality control and the allied arts and sciences. ASQC is recognized as a leader in the development, promotion, and application of quality-related information technology for the quality profession, private sector, government, and academia. ASQC recognizes that continuous quality improvement will help in favorably repositioning U.S. goods and services in the international marketplace.

Board of Overseers

The Board of Overseers advises the Department of Commerce on the Award. The board is appointed by the secretary of commerce and comprises distinguished leaders from all sectors of the U.S. economy. The board evaluates all aspects of the Award program, including the adequacy of the criteria and processes for making awards. An important part of the board's responsibility is to assess how well the Award is serving the national interest. Accordingly, the board makes recommendations to the secretary of commerce and to the director of NIST regarding changes and improvements in the Award program.

Board of Examiners

The Board of Examiners evaluates Award applications, prepares feedback reports, and makes Award recommendations to the director of NIST. It is made up of quality experts, primarily from the private sector. Members are selected by NIST through a competitive application process. For 1992, the board consisted of more than 250 members. Of these, nine served as judges, and approximately fifty served as senior examiners. All members of this board take part in an examiner preparation course.

In addition to their application review responsibilities, members of the Board of Examiners contribute significantly to building awareness of the importance of quality and to information-transfer activities. Many of these activities involve the hundreds of professional, trade, community, and state organizations to which the board members belong.

Award Recipients

The recipients of the Award have shared information on their successful quality strategies with hundreds of thousands of companies, educational institutions, government agencies, health care organizations, and others. By sharing their strategies, Award recipients have made enormous contributions to building awareness of the importance of quality to improving national competitiveness. This sharing has encourage many other organizations to undertake their own quality improvement efforts.

Figure 1 lists the Award winners from 1988 to 1993.

Two

How to Use
This Manual

This manual is designed to serve as an easy-to-use guidebook for individual employees or employee teams to assess and score their organization's quality efforts. It can be used to provide a quality check for an organization's continuous-improvement efforts. It can help employees understand what the Baldrige criteria are asking. It provides a template for an organization's self-assessment and strategic planning efforts, as well as guidance for employees and employee teams to score their departments or total organization in ninety-one areas. It serves as an annual benchmark for improvement, and it helps employees assess their organization's readiness to apply for the Baldrige Award or Baldrige-based industry, city, or state awards. In addition, this manual can be used to help employees collect organizational data to write their quality-award application. The following nine steps explain how this manual can be useful in simplifying the Baldrige Award assessment process for your organization.

Steps to Successful Manual Use

Step 1: Form Assessment Teams

The first step in using this manual is to identify a group of individuals who have an interest in better understanding and using the Baldrige criteria as a template for improving their organization.

After these individuals have been identified, it is time to select and form assessment teams. A team should have from three to five members, who represent different levels of employees throughout the organization. A single assessment team can be formed in smaller organizations to assess all seven Baldrige categories, but in larger organizations it is recommended that several assessment teams be formed to assess each of the categories. Figure 2 is an example of a team's composition representing different employee levels in a larger organization.

Figure 2.   Assessment team composition

Team 1 Leadership	Team 2 Information & analysis	Team 3 Strategic quality planning
• CEO, president or senior VP (team leader) • Director of legal • Director of PR • Manager, operations • Line employee	• VP, MIS (team leader) • Director of MIS • Manager • Supervisor • Line Employee	• VP, strategic planning (team leader) • Director • Manager • Supervisor • Line employee
Team 4 Human resources development & management process	Team 5 Management of process quality	Team 6 Quality & operational results
• VP, human resources (team leader) • Director • Manager • Supervisor • Line employee	• VP, quality (team leader) • Director • Manager • Supervisor • Line employee	• VP, operations (team leader) • Director • Manager • Supervisor • Line employee
	Team 7 Customer focus & satisfaction	
	• VP, marketing (team leader) • Director • Manager • Supervisor • Line employee	

After the teams have been formed, the entire assessment process can take from as little as a month to as much as two months to complete.

Step 2:   Read Baldrige Criteria

After the teams have been formed, members should read the Baldrige Award criteria that appear throughout this manual at the beginning of each of the twenty-eight items. Under each new item summary the Baldrige criteria appear under the heading *Areas to Address.*

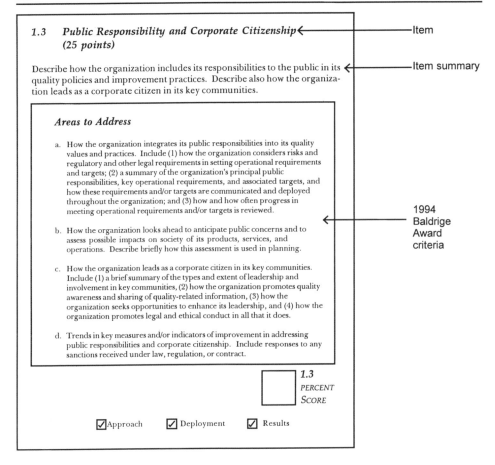

The criteria have been reproduced as they appear in the *1994 Baldrige Award Criteria* booklet. The Baldrige notes have been eliminated but incorporated into the simplified questions throughout the manual.

Facing each of the twenty-eight *Areas to Address* is a page for note taking. Here the assessment team members can record ideas, questions, assignments, and the like.

Step 3:　Ask Simplified Questions

Following each *Areas to Address* page of the manual are questions based on the Baldrige criteria. This manual reduces all Baldrige criteria to simple questions so they are more understandable and user-friendly. This allows a clearer and more precise organizational assessment to be conducted.

The questions are to be asked of different levels of employees throughout the organization. The assessment team should divide this task among its members.

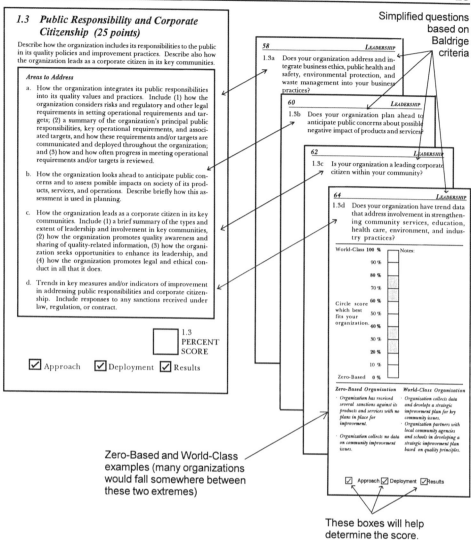

Simplified questions based on Baldrige criteria

Zero-Based and World-Class examples (many organizations would fall somewhere between these two extremes)

These boxes will help determine the score.

Step 4: Determine Score

Before recording answers to the questions, review the examples of *zero-based* organizations and *world-class* organizations that appear on the bottom third of the page. (These two terms are defined in the Glossary.)

Based on the questions and the answers received from employees, determine where the organization would score from 0 percent to 100 percent. To help the assessment team determine the organization's percentage score, Scoring Guidelines and Scoring Profiles are presented in Chapter 3.

Below each question at the bottom of the page appear three boxes, labelled Approach, Deployment, and Results. These boxes will aid in assessing the kinds of information and/or data the question requires.

Step 5:   Make Notes

In the middle of the page under each question is a note section for recording answers to the questions given by employees as they are being interviewed by the assessment team.

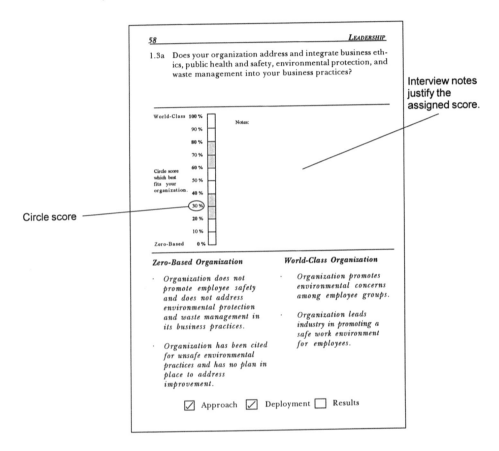

Step 6:   Score the Question

Now it is time to score the question. After rereading the question, reviewing the notes, and comparing zero-based and world-class examples, the assessor should circle the score that best fits the organization.

Step 7:   List Comments for Strengths and Improvement

On the opposing page, the question is restated. After reviewing the score and notes list comments, highlights, strengths, and opportunities for improvement that support the score. All comments should be written in short, clear, sentence form.

Comments should be written
in complete sentences.

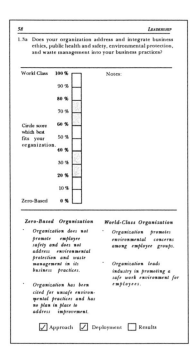
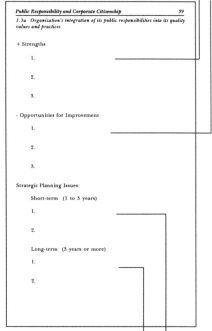

List short-term and
longer-term strategic
planning issues.

Step 8: List Strategic Planning Issues

After reviewing the notes, strengths, and opportunities for improvement, the assessment team should select and list any short-term and long-term strategic planning issues. These data can be used later when developing a strategic plan for the organization.

Step 9: Score Assessment Items

The assessment is broken down into seven Baldrige categories:

  1.0. Leadership
  2.0. Information and Analysis
  3.0. Strategic Quality Planning
  4.0. Human resources Development and Management
  5.0. Management of Process Quality
  6.0. Quality and Operational Results,
  7.0. Customer Focus and Satisfaction.

These seven categories are divided into twenty-eight assessment items (i.e., 1.1, 1.2, . . . 2.1, 2.2, . . .) and the 28 assessment items are broken down into ninety-one areas (i.e., 1.1a, 1.1b, . . . 1.1d . . .).

The percent score is reflective of the strengths and opportunities for improvement of the areas within each assessment item. Thus throughout the assessment all twenty-eight items will obtain a percent score. All assessment item scores will be transferred to the Summary of Assessment Items score sheet located at the end of this manual.

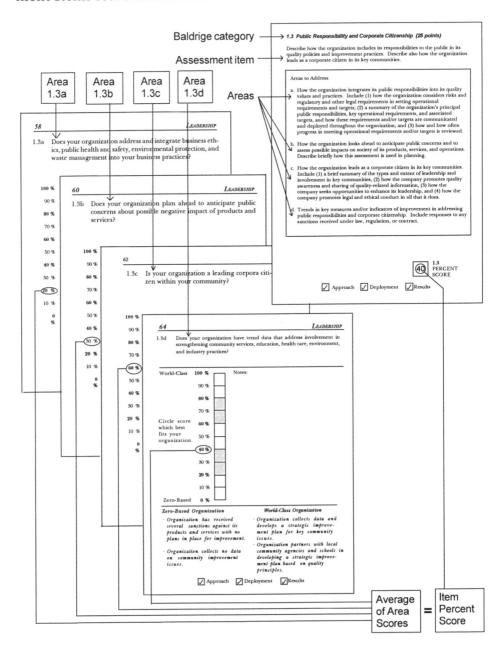

Three

Assessment
Scoring System

The Baldrige scoring system is based on three evaluation dimensions: (1) approach, (2) deployment, and (3) results. All three dimensions should be considered before assigning a percentage score. In addition, each of the twenty-eight items and ninety-one areas assessed in this manual has a scoring profile to help facilitate the scoring process.[1]

The Three Evaluation Dimensions

Approach

Approach refers to the methods the organization uses to achieve purposes addressed in the assessment items. The scoring criteria used to evaluate approaches include one or more of the following, as appropriate:

- The appropriateness of the methods, tools, and techniques to the requirements
- The effectiveness of the use of methods, tools, and techniques
- The degree to which the approach is systematic, integrated, and consistently applied
- The degree to which the approach embodies effective evaluation/improvement cycles
- The degree to which the approach is based upon quantitative information that is objective and reliable
- The degree to which the approach is prevention-based
- The indicators of unique and innovative approaches, including significant and effective new adaptations of tools and techniques used in other applications or types of businesses

---

1. *Source*: 1993 Malcolm Baldrige National Quality Award examiners' course training manual.

17

Deployment

Deployment refers to the extent to which the approaches are applied to all relevant areas and activities addressed and implied in the Assessment Items.

The scoring criteria used to evaluate deployment include one or more of the following, as appropriate:

- The appropriate and effective application by all work units to all processes and activities
- The appropriate and effective application to all product and service features
- The appropriate and effective application to all transactions and interactions with customers, suppliers of goods and services, and the public

Results

Results refers to outcomes and effects in achieving the purposes addressed and implied in the assessment items. The scoring criteria used to evaluate results include one or more of the following:

- The quality and performance levels demonstrated together with their importance
- The rate of quality and performance improvement
- The breadth of quality and performance improvement
- The demonstration of sustained improvement
- The comparison with industry and world leaders
- The organization's ability to show that improvements derive from its quality practices and actions

The percent scores range from a low of zero percent for a zero-based organization to a high of 100 percent for a world-class organization. An organization can be zero percent in some areas and 100 percent (world-class) in others. The *anchor point* is 50 percent, which is the middle of the range. Many U.S. organizations fall below the 50 percent anchor point. It is considered to be good, but certainly below what an organization that is striving to be best-in-class within its industry would score.

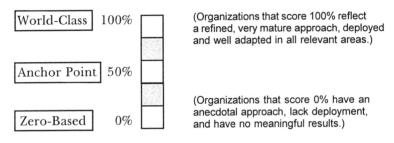

World-Class	100%		(Organizations that score 100% reflect a refined, very mature approach, deployed and well adapted in all relevant areas.)
Anchor Point	50%		
Zero-Based	0%		(Organizations that score 0% have an anecdotal approach, lack deployment, and have no meaningful results.)

Approach and Deployment

Approach and deployment are considered together. This is because without deployment, an approach would merely represent an idea or a plan. Because the Baldrige criteria are based heavily upon "successful quality strategies," they advocate approaches that are actually implemented and deployed.

The following scoring guidelines will assist the assessment team.

SCORING GUIDELINES[2]

	Approach/deployment	Results
World-Class 100%	• A very strong, fact-based improvement process approach, fully deployed	• Excellent current performance in most areas • Strong evidence of industry and benchmark leadership
80	• A sound, systematic approach and deployment in most areas of organization, strong integration with strategic plan • Fact-based improvement process	• Currrent performance is good to excellent in most areas • Performance evaluated against competitive comparisons and benchmarks
60	• A sound, systematic approach and deployment in primary areas of organization • More emphasis on improvement than on reaction to problems	• Improvement trends reported in many to most areas
40	• No main gaps in deployment • A sound, systematic approach	• Improvement trends reported in some areas
20	• Major gaps in deployment • Beginning of a systematic approach • No evidence of systematic approach	• Few or no results reported • Early stages of developing trends
Zero-Based 0		

2. *Source:* Baldrige 1994 Award criteria booklet.

Scoring Profiles

Each of the seven Baldrige categories is profiled into five percentile ranges.[3]

1.0 Leadership   (95 points)

100–80%

. Senior executives are visibly involved in total quality management (TQM).
. Senior leaders are involved and encourage teams to be formed throughout the organization and to focus on continuous improvement.
. Senior leadership communicates organization's quality policies and vision with employees, customers, and suppliers.
. Senior leadership advocates participative management throughout the organization.
. Senior leadership reflects the organization's commitment to public health, safety, environmental protection, organizational values, and continuous improvement efforts.

80–60%

. Most senior executives are visibly involved in promoting quality throughout the organization.
. Senior executives meet with employee groups/teams, critical suppliers, and customers on quality issues.
. Commitment to public responsibility and corporate citizenship is deployed throughout the organization by senior leaders.
. Management behavior at all levels of the organization reflects quality as a major priority for the organization.
. Senior leaders communicate the organization's quality policies, vision, and mission to employees, suppliers, and customers.

60–40%

. Senior leaders share quality values with employees, customers, and suppliers.
. Managers' performance is evaluated against measurable quality strategies.
. Senior leaders are committed to public responsibility and corporate citizenship.

---

3. *Source:* 1994 President's Quality Award Program, *Quality Improvement Prototype Award Criteria Manual*, Federal Quality Institute.

- Participative management is practiced in many parts of the organization.
- Senior leaders support short- and long-term strategic quality improvement.

40–20%

- A few senior leaders and managers support and are involved in the organization's quality improvement efforts.
- Managers and supervisors are encouraged to become involved in the organization's quality improvement efforts
- Communication within the organization is usually vertical (top down); no cooperation across departments is encouraged.
- The organization's quality policies reflect commitment to public responsibility and corporate citizenship.
- Continuous improvement is practiced in some parts of the organization.

20–0%

- Senior leaders are beginning to support the quality process.
- Quality practices are not understood in some parts of the organization.
- Senior leaders have not fully developed their quality vision, nor is there a quality plan in place.
- Senior leadership does not get involved with suppliers, customers, and employees in sharing the organization's quality vision.
- Public responsibility and corporate citizenship are of no concern to senior management.

2.0 Information and Analysis (75 points)

100–80%

- Quality-related data available for critical processes are used to produce products/services.
- Processes and technology that ensure timely, accurate, valid and useful data collection for process owners are used throughout the organization
- Data are analyzed organization wide by employee teams that translate it into usable information to ensure continuous quality improvement.
- Competitive comparisons and benchmarking information and data are used to help drive continuous improvement.
- Quality-related data are integrated and distributed to process owners throughout the organization.

80–60%

- Employees have rapid access to data in most parts of the organization.
- Processes and technologies are used across most of the organization to ensure that data are complete, timely, accurate, valid, and useful.
- Comparative data are collected, analyzed, and translated into usable information to support decision making and planning.
- Most critical processes have data on quality, timeliness, and productivity.
- Measures exist that relate to the organization's strategic objectives for most products/services.

60–40%

- Benchmark and comparative data are collected on some products, services, and processes.
- Processes and technologies are used across many parts of the organization to ensure that data are complete, timely, accurate, valid, and useful.
- Employees have access to data in many parts of the organization.
- Many critical processes have data on quality, timeliness, and productivity.
- Measures exist that relate to the organization's strategic objectives for many products/services.

40–20%

- Data exist for some critical products/services and processes.
- Data on many major processes are limited.
- Data are collected on some customers and suppliers.
- A centralized group analyzes data; employee teams are not used for data analysis.
- Limited process controls are in place to ensure that data analysis is used to drive improvement within the organization.

20–0%

- Data received for comparison appears anecdotal.
- Data received are used primarily for reporting purposes, not for improvement.
- Limited data are used for a select few critical processes.
- None or very little customer or supplier data are used for improvement.
- Data analysis is in the beginning stages of use for the organization's improvement efforts.

3.0 *Strategic Quality Planning* (60 points)

100–80%

- Strategic planning is used to develop quality improvement goals throughout the organization.
- All employee levels give input to the strategic planning process.
- Employees, customers, and suppliers are fully involved in the planning process.
- All management levels are actively involved in the planning process.
- The strategic planning process includes short-term and long-term plans based on key quality data, customer and employee survey data, supplier and benchmark data that are deployed throughout the organization.

80–60%

- Strategic plans for quality improvement relating to mission, vision, and values are established across the organization.
- The organization uses a broad planning process that involves employees, customers, and suppliers.
- The strategic planning process includes short-term and long-term plans based on key quality data, customer and employee survey data, and supplier and benchmark data that are deployed throughout the organization.
- Senior management provides input and approves the strategic plan.
- Operational plans are developed throughout the organization that are linked to the master strategic plan; managers are held accountable for meeting strategic goals.

60–40%

- Operational plans developed at key suborganizational levels link with the strategic plan.
- Managers at all levels are held accountable for attaining major objectives.
- The organization involves employees, suppliers, and customers in the planning process.
- The strategic planning process includes short-term and long-term plans based on some quality data, customer and employee survey data, and supplier and benchmark data that are deployed throughout most parts of the organization.
- The strategic planning process is deployed across the organization and approved by senior management.

40–20%

- Strategic goals are established for key functional areas of the organization.
- A strategic planning process is in place within the organization.
- Senior executives approve the strategic plan.
- Some customers and suppliers are involved in the strategic planning process.
- Management provides customer data for the strategic planning process.

20–0%

- None to very few customers or suppliers are involved in the organization's strategic planning process.
- Employees at lower levels of the organization are not involved in the planning process.
- Strategic planning is neither mentioned nor understood throughout the organization.
- The organization's plan is developed by senior staff, with no input from employees, suppliers, or customers.
- The strategic plan has no customer involvement or customer focus.

4.0 Human Resource Development and Management (150 points)

100–80%

- The organization has fully implemented and deployed employee growth and development plans, education, training, and empowerment, with measurable results.
- The organization has documented favorable trends regarding the percentage of employees recognized for individual and team contributions; recognition is tied to the organization's quality goals and strategic plan.
- There have been positive trends within the past few years of team involvement regarding improved work processes across the organization.
- Employee innovations, cross-functional teams, and natural work groups are encouraged throughout the organization.
- The organization is highly sensitive to employee well-being and satisfaction.

80–60%

- Senior management and most middle management support employee involvement, contributions, and teamwork.

- Teams and employee work groups feel a strong sense of empower-ment and practice innovations across most parts of the organization.
- Employees have rapid access to data through their computer networks in most parts of the organization.
- Employee idea sharing is encouraged and acted upon by man-agement across most parts of the organization.
- The organization maintains a work environment conducive to the well-being and growth of most employees.

60–40%

- Employees are empowered throughout many parts of the orga-nization and encouraged to become members of cross-functional and problem solving teams.
- The organization has a documented strategic plan in place for employee development, education, and skills training.
- Employee recognition is tied to the organization's quality goals and objectives.
- Management in many parts of the organization supports teams and team development.
- The organization is sensitive to employee well-being and morale.

40–20%

- Employee empowerment is not encouraged throughout the organization.
- Rewards and recognition are not fully deployed among all em-ployee levels; they are more focused on individual, as opposed to team, contributions.
- Not all employee development and training initiatives are con-nected with the organization's quality plans and objectives.
- Managers in some parts of the organization support employee involvement and empowerment.
- The organization not consistently supportive of a work environ-ment conducive to the well-being and growth of the employees.

20–0%

- The organization does not offer training on a consistent basis.
- Few employees are empowered or work in teams within the organization.
- Employee rewards and recognition appear not to be focused on the organization's quality plan and goals for continuous improvement.
- Employee development is not a priority initiative within the organization.

- Some managers support employee involvement and participative management.

5.0 Management of Process Quality   (140 points)

100–80%

- Processes are documented and controlled across the organization.
- Systematic approaches are used throughout the organization to ensure shortened cycle-time and consistent products and services.
- Critical supplier partnerships are formed or supplier certification programs are in place to ensure consistency of all processes throughout the organization.
- Periodic assessments of critical processes are conducted.
- Analytic problem-solving tools are used throughout the organization to identify and solve process problems.

80–60%

- Processes are documented and controlled across most parts of the organization.
- Systematic approaches are used throughout most parts of the organization to ensure shortened cycle-time and consistent products and services.
- Supplier quality is a main consideration when selecting critical suppliers.
- Comprehensive assessments are conducted consistently throughout the organization to ensure that all processes are meeting customer requirements.
- Analytic problem-solving tools are used in most parts of the organization to identify and solve process problems.

60–40%

- The organization uses customer data (e.g., survey data, focus groups) to design processes for new/improved products and services in many parts of the organization.
- Critical suppliers are required to meet documented standards in many parts of the organization.
- Problem-solving tools are used in many parts of the organization.
- Process assessments are conducted in many parts of the organization.
- Standardized preventive measures to ensure quality products/services are used in many parts of the organization.

40–20%

- In most parts of the organization, appraisal is emphasized as opposed to prevention.
- Cost is the primary consideration in choosing suppliers.
- Quality assessments of core processes are conducted only when processes are consistently out of control.
- Problem-solving tools are used in some parts of the organization.
- Some customer input is sought to improve processes.

20–0%

- Systematic approaches to ensure reduced cycle time and improved processes are delegated to the quality assurance manager.
- No customer or supplier input is sought to improve the organization's core processes.
- Suppliers are not considered partners-in-quality within the organization.
- Very few or no problem-solving tools are used to identify and solve process problems.
- The organization is in an appraisal mode rather than a prevention mode.

6.0 Quality and Operational Results (180 points)

100–80%

- Customer satisfaction surveys have shown positive trends over the past two to three years.
- Supplier data have shown improvement over the past two to three years.
- There have been positive results in reduced cycle-time and productivity improvement in products and services across the organization over the past two to three years.
- Improvement plans are in place in areas of the organization that show negative trends.
- Business and support services have shown improved results and positive trends over the past two to three years.

80–60%

- Most operational performance levels have demonstrated positive results over the past two to three years.
- Results indicate some suppliers have improved over the past two to three years.

- Results reflect improvement in cycle-time and operational performance.
- Benchmark results reveal that the organization is leading competition in several core processes.
- Key measures of business and support services reflect principal quality, productivity, cycle time, and cost results have improved over the past two to three years in most parts of the organization.

60–40%

- Customer satisfaction surveys have reflected positive results over the past two to three years.
- Critical suppliers are meeting quality standards, with a few having shown positive results over the past two years.
- Benchmarks are conducted within key areas of the organization, and benchmark results are documented.
- Key measures of operational, product, and service results are captured in critical areas of the organization; positive results have been reflected over the past two to three years.
- Competitive comparisons are made within the organization that reflect positive one-to-two year results.

40–20%

- Product/service measures reflect improved trends.
- Customer satisfaction surveys reflect improvement.
- Some suppliers are meeting the organization's documented quality standards.
- Improved results in cycle-time and improved products/services are documented in some parts of the organization.
- Measurement is not fully deployed across the organization.

20–0%

- There is only anecdotal evidence of improvement.
- Customer satisfaction is not measured.
- Improvements are measured in few if any parts of the organization.
- Supplier improvement is not measured or considered.
- No benchmarking is conducted.

7.0 Customer Focus and Satisfaction (300 points)

100–80%

- Customer surveys, focus groups, and exit interviews are used to determine customer satisfaction, repurchase intentions, and customer satisfaction relative to competitors.

- Management is actively focused on ensuring an internal/external customer focus throughout the organization.
- Customer-contact training is required throughout the organization for employees who interface with customers.
- The organization promotes trust and confidence in its products/services.
- The organization is continuously determining near-term and longer-term customer requirements and expectations.

80–60%

- Effective feedback systems are in place to obtain critical customer data for continuous improvement.
- Management promotes and deploys an internal/external customer focus throughout the organization.
- Senior management is approachable by customers.
- Specific customer-contact training is in place.
- Logistical support is in place for customer-contact employees.

60–40%

- Customer-survey data are deployed throughout the organization to drive continuous improvement in products/services.
- Customer-contact employees are trained.
- An internal/external customer focus is promoted throughout the organization
- Customer focus and satisfaction issues tie in with the organization's near-term and longer-term strategic plans.
- Effective systems are in place in many products/services linking internal/external customer feedback to employee teams.

40–20%

- Most internal/external customers are identified; needs and expectations are not determined through a systematic process.
- Some customer groups are segmented.
- Customer-service standards are revised periodically for some products/services.
- Senior management is not always accessible by customers.
- Future customer expectations are not determined or considered in the organization's near-term and longer-term planning process.

20–0%

- Few if any customer-service standards have been established by the organization.

- The customer service focus is on problem solving.
- Customer feedback is not always considered when developing or improving products/services.
- Customer complaints are the major method for obtaining customer feedback.
- The organization does not promote trust and confidence in its products/services.

PART II
THE CATEGORIES

1.0

Leadership

Total section value: 95 points

The *Leadership* category examines senior executives' personal leadership and involvement in creating and sustaining a customer focus and clear and visible quality values. Also examined is how the quality values are integrated into the organization's management system and reflected in how the organization addresses its public responsibilities.

1.1 Notes

1.1 Senior Executive Leadership (45 points)

Describe the senior executives' leadership, personal involvement, and visibility in developing and maintaining an environment for quality excellence.

Areas to Address

a. Senior executives' leadership, personal involvement, and visibility in quality-related activities of the organization. Include (1) creating and reinforcing a customer focus and quality values, (2) setting expectations and planning, (3) reviewing quality and operational performance, (4) recognizing contributions, and (5) communicating quality values outside the organization.

b. Brief summary of the organization's customer focus and quality values that serve as a basis for consistent understanding and communication within and outside the organization.

c. How senior executives regularly communicate and reinforce the organization's customer focus and quality values with managers and supervisors.

d. How senior executives evaluate and improve the effectiveness of their personal leadership and involvement.

[ ] **1.1** PERCENT SCORE

[✓] Approach [✓] Deployment [ ] Results

1.1a   *To what extent are senior leaders involved in your organization's quality efforts?*

- *Goal Setting*
- *Planning*
- *Reviewing organizational quality performance*
- *Communicating with employees*
- *Recognizing employee contributions*
- *Other activities, including:*
  - *—Learning about quality of domestic and international competitors*
  - *—Meeting with customers and suppliers*
  - *—Participating in teams*

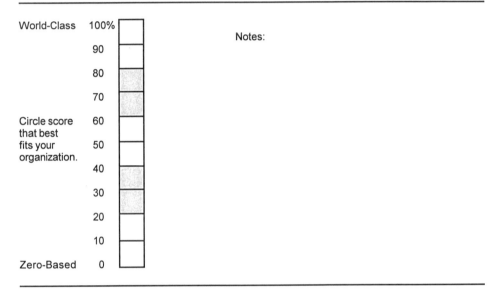

Notes:

Zero-Based Organization	World-Class Organization
• *Not all senior leaders are personally involved in deploying quality-related activities throughout the organization.*	• *Senior leaders are personally and visibly involved in deploying a customer-focused environment for quality excellence throughout the organization.*
• *Senior leaders are not focused on becoming internally customer-driven.*	• *Senior leaders are involved in employee recognition.*

☑ Approach   ☑ Deployment   ☐ Results

1.1a   Senior leaders' personal involvement

+ Strengths

1.

2.

3.

– Opportunities for improvement

1.

2.

3.

Strategic planning issues

Short-term (one to three years)

1.

2.

Long-term (three years or more)

1.

2.

1.1b   *Do senior leaders focus and integrate your organization's quality values when they communicate within and outside your organization?*

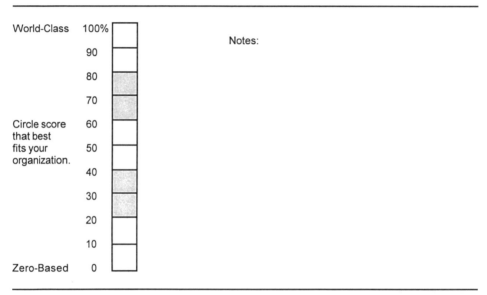

World-Class   100%

90

80

70

Circle score   60
that best
fits your   50
organization.
40

30

20

10

Zero-Based   0

Notes:

Zero-Based Organization	***World-Class Organization***

- *Organization's values are not shared with all suppliers and customers.*

- *Organization's values are not shared with new hires during their orientation.*

- *Organization has published a values statement.*

- *Organization bases quality values on a corporate quality creed, code of business conduct and operating principles, corporate strategy for excellence, mission statement, and supporting guidelines and standards.*

☑ Approach   ☑ Deployment   ☐ Results

1.1b   *Senior leaders' approach to building quality values within and outside organization*

+ Strengths

   1.

   2.

   3.

– Opportunities for improvement

   1.

   2.

   3.

Strategic planning issues

   Short-term (one to three years)

   1.

   2.

   Long-term (three years or more)

   1.

   2.

1.1c   *Do senior leaders communicate your organization's customer orientation and quality values to all levels of management and supervision?*

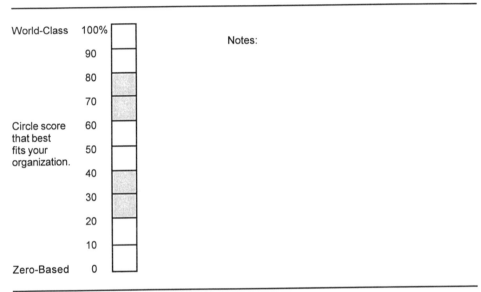

World-Class   100%

90

80

70

Circle score   60
that best
fits your   50
organization.

40

30

20

10

Zero-Based   0

Notes:

Zero-Based Organization	World-Class Organization
• *Senior leadership staff does not communicate quality values throughout the organization consistently.*	• *President or CEO communicates the organization's customer-service orientation and quality values through articles in the employee newsletter, organizational marketing material, and internal/external speeches.*
• *Senior staff does not communicate organization's customer focus and quality values to managers and supervisors.*	• *Customer service training and quality values are taught to managers and supervisors by senior executives.*

☑ Approach   ☑ Deployment   ☐ Results

1.1c   *Senior leaders' communication of quality values to managers and supervisors*

+ Strengths

    1.

    2.

    3.

– Opportunities for improvement

    1.

    2.

    3.

Strategic planning issues

    Short-term (one to three years)

    1.

    2.

    Long-term (three years or more)

    1.

    2.

1.1d   *How do senior leaders evaluate and improve their leadership effectiveness and personal involvement within your organization?*

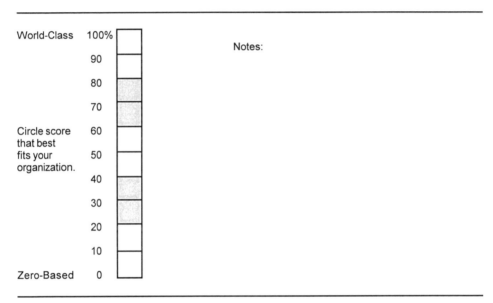

World-Class   100%

Notes:

90

80

70

Circle score   60
that best
fits your   50
organization.

40

30

20

10

Zero-Based   0

Zero-Based Organization

- *Senior leaders do not monitor leadership effectiveness and personal involvement.*

- *Senior leaders have not designed or utilized an evaluation process for their personal leadership improvement.*

World-Class Organization

- *Direct reports rate managers annually with a leadership questionnaire; senior leaders use these data to improve.*

- *Senior leaders have a plan in place to continuously monitor personal involvement with employees, suppliers, and customers.*

☑ Approach   ☑ Deployment   ☐ Results

1.1d   *Senior leadership's evaluation and improvement of leadership effectiveness and personal involvement*

+ Strengths

1.

2.

3.

– Opportunities for improvement

1.

2.

3.

Strategic planning issues

Short-term (one to three years)

1.

2.

Long-term (three years or more)

1.

2.

1.2 Notes

1.2 Management for Quality (25 points)

Describe how the organization's customer focus and quality values are integrated into day-to-day leadership, management, and supervision of all organization units.

Areas to Address

a. How the organization's customer focus and quality values are translated into requirements for all managers and supervisors. Describe (1) their principal roles and responsibilities within their units and (2) their roles and responsibilities in fostering cooperation with other units.

b. How the organization's customer focus and quality values (1.1b) are communicated and reinforced throughout the entire workforce.

c. How overall organization and work-unit quality and operational performance are reviewed. Describe (1) types, frequency, content, and use of reviews and who conducts them and (2) how the organization assists units that are not performing according to plans.

d. How the organization evaluates and improves managers' and supervisors' effectiveness in reinforcing the organization's customer focus and quality values.

1.2
PERCENT
SCORE

☑ Approach   ☑ Deployment   ☐ Results

47

1.2a   *Does your organization hold managers and supervisors account-*
       able for quality? Do you have specific measures and guidelines for
       them based on their level, function, and position?

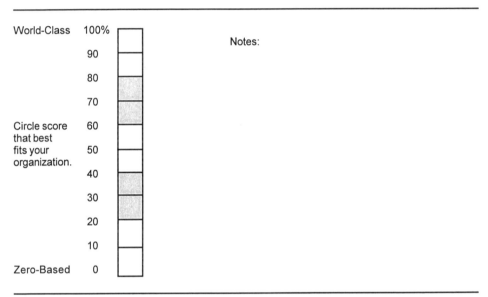

World-Class   100%

              90

              80

              70

Circle score 60
that best
fits your   50
organization.
              40

              30

              20

              10

Zero-Based   0

Notes:

Zero-Based Organization

- *Organization's customer focus and quality values are not fully deployed among all managers and supervisors.*

- *A limited number of managers and supervisors are involved in the organization's quality process.*

World-Class Organization

- *Organization supports employee participation among all managers and supervisors.*

- *Annual performance reviews encourage manager and supervisor involvement in the quality process.*

☑ Approach   ☑ Deployment   ☐ Results

1.2a   Managers and supervisors held accountable for quality within the organization

+ Strengths

   1.

   2.

   3.

– Opportunities for improvement

   1.

   2.

   3.

Strategic planning issues

   Short-term (one to three years)

   1.

   2.

   Long-term (three years or more)

   1.

   2.

1.2b   Are your organization's customer focus and quality values communicated to each employee?

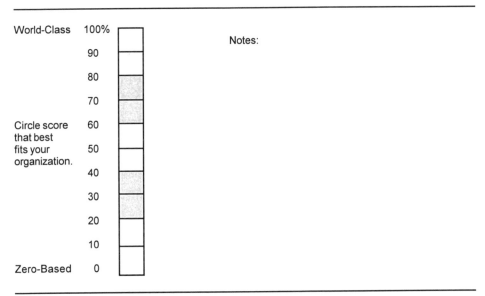

World-Class   100%

90

80

70

Circle score   60
that best
fits your   50
organization.
40

30

20

10

Zero-Based   0

Notes:

Zero-Based Organization

- *No customer focus and quality values are communicated.*

- *Customer focus and quality values communicated to customers only.*

World-Class Organization

- *Customer focus and quality values are communicated to employees on a regular basis.*

- *All employee correspondence, newsletters, staff meetings and corporate videos reflect customer focus and quality values.*

☑ Approach   ☑ Deployment   ☐ Results

1.2b   Communication of customer focus and quality values to employees

+ Strengths

   1.

   2.

   3.

– Opportunities for improvement

   1.

   2.

   3.

Strategic planning issues

   Short-term (one to three years)

   1.

   2.

   Long-term (three years or more)

   1.

   2.

1.2c   *Do your employees have regularly scheduled, frequent meetings during which quality of work (reduction of errors) is reviewed against your organization's plans or goals?*
Is assistance offered to those not performing according to plan?

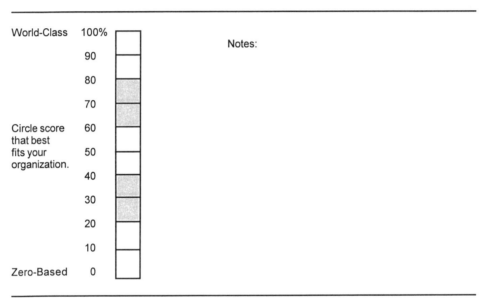

World-Class   100%

90

80

70

Circle score   60
that best
fits your   50
organization.

40

30

20

10

Zero-Based   0

Notes:

Zero-Based Organization

- *Employees are not involved in identifying quality issues and developing strategies.*

- *Organization does not review work unit quality and operational performance.*

World-Class Organization

- *Team quality review meetings are held weekly and monthly with formal agendas.*

- *Review teams are composed of cross-functional members who review daily nonconformers and offer assistance to those not performing according to plan.*

☑ Approach   ☑ Deployment   ☐ Results

1.2c   Reviews of work-unit quality and operational performance con-
*   ducted against the organization's plan*

+ Strengths

   1.

   2.

   3.

– Opportunities for improvement

   1.

   2.

   3.

Strategic planning issues

   Short-term (one to three years)

   1.

   2.

   Long-term (three years or more)

   1.

   2.

1.2d   *Does your organization evaluate managers' and supervisors' reinforcement of customer focus and quality values with their employees?*

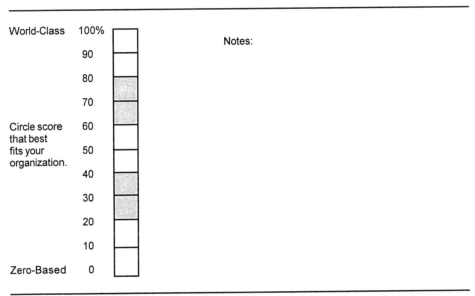

Zero-Based Organization

- *Managers and supervisors are not encouraged to reinforce customer focus and quality values among their employees.*

- *Managers and supervisors do not participate in the organization's quality process.*

World-Class Organization

- *Managers and supervisors are rewarded for implementation of customer focus and quality values among employees who report to them.*

- *Managers and supervisors are encouraged by senior executives to be customer focused in their leadership.*

☑ Approach   ☑ Deployment   ☐ Results

1.2d   *Manager and supervisor reinforcement of organization's customer focus and quality values*

+ Strengths

1.

2.

3.

– Opportunities for improvement

1.

2.

3.

Strategic planning issues

Short-term (one to three years)

1.

2.

Long-term (three years or more)

1.

2.

1.3 Notes

1.3 Public Responsibility and Corporate Citizenship (25 points)

Describe how the organization includes its responsibilities to the public in its quality policies and improvement practices. Describe also how the organization leads as a corporate citizen in its key communities.

Areas to Address

a. How the organization integrates its public responsibilities into its quality values and practices. Include (1) how the organization considers risks and regulatory and other legal requirements in setting operational requirements and targets; (2) a summary of the organization's principal public responsibilities, key operational requirements, and associated targets, and how these requirements and/or targets are communicated and deployed throughout the organization; and (3) how and how often progress in meeting operational requirements and/or targets is reviewed.

b. How the organization looks ahead to anticipate public concerns and to assess possible impacts on society of its products, services, and operations. Describe briefly how this assessment is used in planning.

c. How the organization leads as a corporate citizen in its key communities. Include (1) a brief summary of the types and extent of leadership and involvement in key communities, (2) how the organization promotes quality awareness and sharing of quality-related information, (3) how the organization seeks opportunities to enhance its leadership, and (4) how the organization promotes legal and ethical conduct in all that it does.

d. Trends in key measures and/or indicators of improvement in addressing public responsibilities and corporate citizenship. Include responses to any sanctions received under law, regulation, or contract.

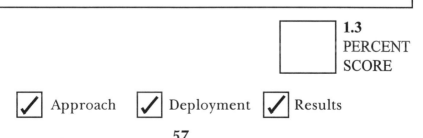

1.3
PERCENT
SCORE

☑ Approach ☑ Deployment ☑ Results

1.3a   Does your organization address and integrate business ethics, public health and safety, environmental protection, and waste management into your business practices?

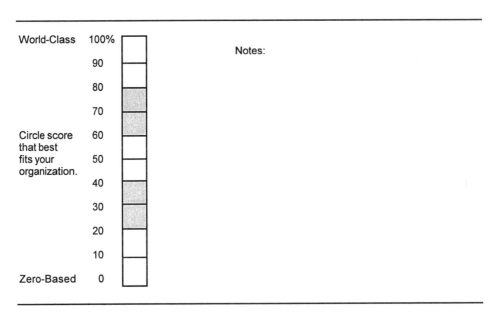

Zero-Based Organization	World-Class Organization
• Organization does not promote employee safety and does not address environmental protection and waste management in its business practices.	• Organization promotes environmental concerns among employee groups.
• Organization has been cited for unsafe environmental practices and has no plan in place to address improvement.	• Organization leads industry in promoting a safe work environment for employees.

☑ Approach   ☑ Deployment   ☐ Results

1.3a   *Organization's integration of its public responsibilities into its quality values and practices*

+ Strengths

1.

2.

3.

– Opportunities for improvement

1.

2.

3.

Strategic planning issues

Short-term (one to three years)

1.

2.

Long-term (three years or more)

1.

2.

*1.3b   Does your organization plan ahead to anticipate public concerns
about possible negative impact of products and services?*

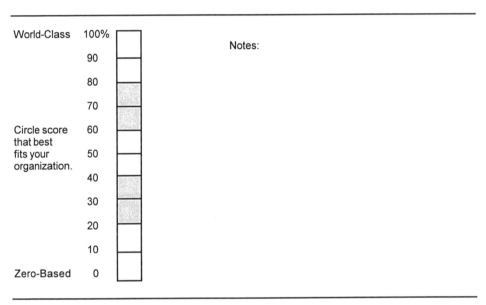

Zero-Based Organization	World-Class Organization
• *Organization never considers public concerns about its products and services.*	• *Organization surveys segments of community that are impacted by its products, services, and operations.*
• *Negative publicity about organization's ethics and environmental and safety practices are of no concern to senior leaders.*	• *Organization establishes community focus groups and acts as a partner with them on establishing community environmental and safety practices.*

☑ Approach   ☑ Deployment   ☐ Results

1.3b　*Organizational plan in place to anticipate ethical, environmental, and safety concerns from the community*

+ Strengths

　1.

　2.

　3.

– Opportunities for improvement

　1.

　2.

　3.

Strategic planning issues

　Short-term (one to three years)

　1.

　2.

　Long-term (three years or more)

　1.

　2.

*1.3c   Is your organization a leading corporate citizen within your
community?*

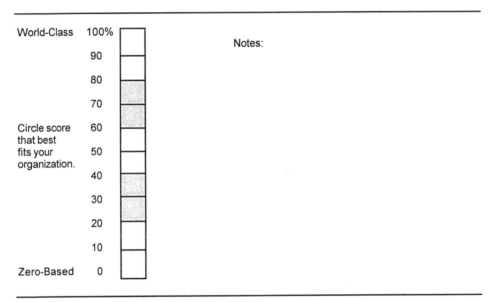

World-Class   100%

Notes:

90

80

70

Circle score   60
that best
fits your   50
organization.
40

30

20

10

Zero-Based   0

Zero-Based Organization

- *Organization does not share
quality policies and improvement
practices with the community.*

- *Organization does not get involved and try to strengthen
community services, education,
health care, environment and
practices of industry associates.*

World-Class Organization

- *Employees are encouraged to promote
total quality management in local,
state, national, and industry
organizations.*

- *Various employee levels conduct
community and industry tours within
the organization.*

☑ Approach   ☑ Deployment   ☐ Results

1.3c　Organization's leadership as a corporate citizen within the community

+ Strengths

　1.

　2.

　3.

– Opportunities for improvement

　1.

　2.

　3.

Strategic planning issues

　Short-term (one to three years)

　1.

　2.

　Long-term (three years or more)

　1.

　2.

1.3d   *Does your organization have trend data that address involvement in strengthening community services, education, health care, environment, and industry practices?*
Has your organization received any sanctions against its products or services within the past three years?

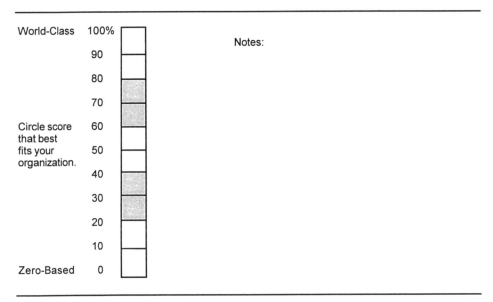

World-Class   100%

90

80

70

Circle score   60
that best
fits your   50
organization.
40

30

20

10

Zero-Based   0

Notes:

Zero-Based Organization	*World-Class Organization*
• *Organization has received several sanctions against its products and services with no plans in place for improvement.*	• *Organization collects data and develops a strategic improvement plan for key community issues that relate directly to its products and services.*
• *Organization collects no data on community improvement issues.*	• *Organization partners with local community agencies and schools in developing a strategic improvement plan based on quality principles.*

☐ Approach   ☐ Deployment   ☑ Results

*1.3d   Organization's collection of key measures to ensure community
improvement*

+ Strengths

1.

2.

3.

– Opportunities for improvement

1.

2.

3.

Strategic planning issues

Short-term (one to three years)

1.

2.

Long-term (three years or more)

1.

2.

Source of the following: 1994 Award Criteria;
Malcolm Baldrige National Quality Award examination
items and notes are excerpted throughout
Measuring Up to the Baldrige.

2.0

Information and Analysis

Total section value: 75 points

The *Information and Analysis* category examines the scope, validity, analysis, management, and use of data and information to drive quality excellence and improve competitive performance. Also examined is the adequacy of the organization's data, information, and analysis system to support improvement of the organization's customer focus, products, services, and internal operations.

2.1 Notes

2.1 Scope and Management of Quality and Performance (15 points)

Describe the organization's selection and management of data and information used for planning, day-to-day management, and evaluation of quality and operational performance.

Areas to Address

a. Criteria for selecting data and information for use in quality and operational performance improvement. List key types of data and information used, and briefly outline the principal roles of each type in improving quality and operational performance. Include (1) customer-related; (2) product and service performance; (3) internal operations and performance, including business and support services and employee-related; (4) supplier performance; and (5) cost and financial.

b. How reliability, consistency, and rapid access to data are ensured throughout the organization. If applicable, describe how software accuracy and reliability are assured.

c. How the organization evaluates and improves the scope and management of data and information. Include (1) review and update, (2) shortening the cycle from data gathering to access, (3) broadening access to all those requiring data for day-to-day management and improvement, and (4) aligning data and information with process improvement plans and needs.

☐ **2.1 PERCENT SCORE**

☑ Approach ☑ Deployment ☐ Results

69

2.1a   *Within your organization, do you measure data that all employees can understand?*
Will that data help them provide better service to your customers? Categories include (1) customer-related, (2) product and service performance, (3) employee-related, (4) supplier performance, and (5) cost and financial.

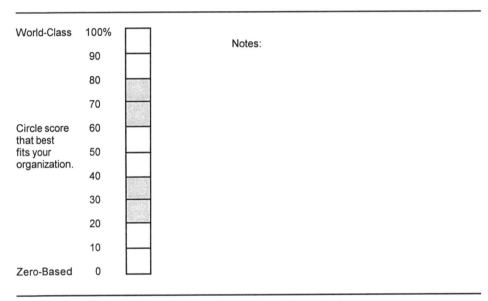

World-Class   100%

90

80

70

Circle score that best fits your organization.   60

50

40

30

20

10

Zero-Based   0

Notes:

Zero-Based Organization	World-Class Organization
• No quality-related data are measured.	• Quality-related data are integrated and distributed throughout the organization.
• Data that are measured are not presented in a user-friendly format for employees to understand.	• Data gathering supports organization's quality efforts.

☑ Approach   ☑ Deployment   ☐ Results

2.1a   *Criteria for selection of data used for planning, day-to-day man-*
         agement, and evaluation of quality

+ Strengths

   1.

   2.

   3.

– Opportunities for improvement

   1.

   2.

   3.

Strategic planning issues

   Short-term (one to three years)

   1.

   2.

   Long-term (three years or more)

   1.

   2.

2.1b   *How is reliable data that your organization uses disseminated to your employees on a timely basis?*

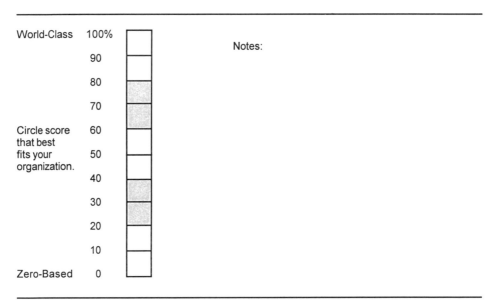

World-Class   100%

90

80

70

Circle score   60
that best
fits your   50
organization.

40

30

20

10

Zero-Based   0

Notes:

Zero-Based Organization

- *No process or technology exists to track, monitor, or retrieve quality-related data for employees.*

- *Data are not disseminated to employees within various departments.*

World-Class Organization

- *Information systems are fully integrated and user-friendly for information exchange and dissemination throughout the organization.*

- *Each employee has rapid access to data through the personal computer located in employee's work area.*

☑ Approach   ☑ Deployment   ☐ Results

2.1b   *Processes ensuring reliability and rapid access to data used*
       throughout organization

+ Strengths

   1.

   2.

   3.

– Opportunities for improvement

   1.

   2.

   3.

Strategic planning issues

   Short-term (one to three years)

   1.

   2.

   Long-term (three years or more)

   1.

   2.

2.1c   *How do you evaluate and improve the scope and quality of your data collection? That is, how do you shorten the cycle time from data gathering to employee access?*

World-Class   100%

90

80

70

Circle score   60
that best
fits your   50
organization.

40

30

20

10

Zero-Based   0

Notes:

Zero-Based Organization   **World-Class Organization**

- *No system exists for data collection.*

- *No strategic plan is in place to prioritize and coordinate data collection throughout the organization.*

- *Continuous-improvement methods are utilized to improve the scope and quality of data collection throughout the organization.*

- *Data and information collection are aligned with organization's cycle-time reduction plans and needs.*

☑ Approach   ☑ Deployment   ☐ Results

2.1c   *Evaluation and improvement of data scope and quality of data collection*

+ Strengths

   1.

   2.

   3.

– Opportunities for improvement

   1.

   2.

   3.

Strategic planning issues

   Short-term (one to three years)

   1.

   2.

   Long-term (three years or more)

   1.

   2.

2.2 Notes

2.2 Competitive Comparisons and Benchmarking (20 points)

Describe the organization's processes, current sources and scope, and uses of competitive comparisons and benchmarking information and data to support improvement of quality and operational performance.

Areas to Address

a. How competitive comparisons and benchmarking information and data are used to help drive improvement of quality and operational performance. Describe (1) how needs are determined and (2) criteria for seeking competitive comparisons and benchmarking information—from within and outside the organization's industry.

b. Brief summary of current scope, sources, and principal uses of each type of competitive comparisons and benchmarking information and data. Include (1) customer-related; (2) product and service quality; (3) internal operations and performance, including business and support services and employee-related; and (4) supplier performance.

c. How competitive comparisons and benchmarking information and data are used to improve understanding of processes, to encourage breakthrough approaches, and to set "stretch" targets.

d. How the organization evaluates and improves its overall processes for selecting and using competitive comparisons and benchmarking information and data to improve planning and operational performance.

☐ 2.2 PERCENT SCORE

☑ Approach ☑ Deployment ☐ Results

2.2a   Does your organization use competitive and benchmark data to
        drive improvement of quality and operational performance?

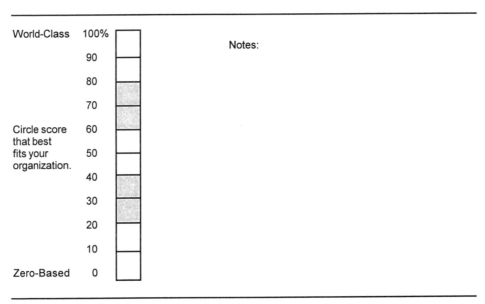

Zero-Based Organization	World-Class Organization
• Benchmarking process is neither understood nor used.	• Continuously looking for best-in-class processes to benchmark in order to make organization world-class.
• All data received for comparison are anecdotal.	• Organization has developed a benchmark process for teams to follow.

☑ Approach   ☑ Deployment   ☐ Results

*2.2a   Organization's use of competitive and benchmark data for
        improvement*

+ Strengths

   1.

   2.

   3.

– Opportunities for improvement

   1.

   2.

   3.

Strategic planning issues

   Short-term (one to three years)

   1.

   2.

   Long-term (three years or more)

   1.

   2.

2.2b   *How many different sources of competitive and benchmark data does your organization have?*

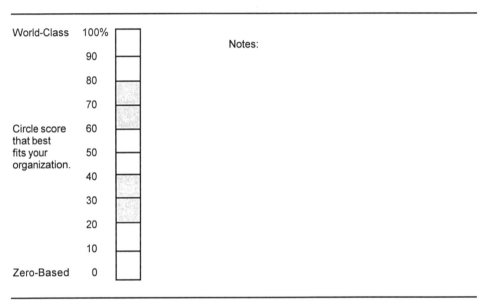

World-Class   100%

Notes:

90

80

70

Circle score   60
that best
fits your   50
organization.

40

30

20

10

Zero-Based   0

Zero-Based Organization

- *Comparative data on competition is based upon subjective opinion of a few individuals.*

- *Limited benchmarking, or none, is conducted.*

World-Class Organization

- *Organization has in place a thorough, ongoing search for best-in-class processes.*

- *Organization conducts benchmarks to improve product and service delivery cycle time, reduction of internal processes, supplier performance, and internal operations and performance.*

☑ Approach   ☑ Deployment   ☐ Results

2.2*b*   *Current scope and uses of competitive comparisons and*
         benchmark data

+ Strengths

  1.

  2.

  3.

– Opportunities for improvement

  1.

  2.

  3.

Strategic planning issues

  Short-term (one to three years)

  1.

  2.

  Long-term (three years or more)

  1.

  2.

2.2c   Does your organization use benchmarking to improve critical
       processes, encourage innovative approaches, and set stretch targets?

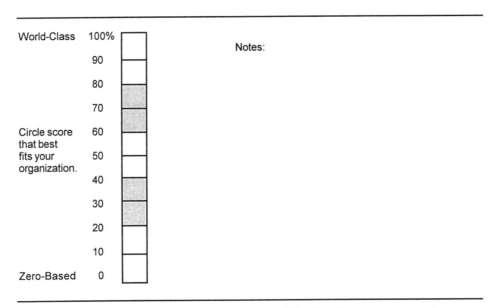

World-Class   100%

              90

              80

              70

Circle score 60
that best
fits your   50
organization.
              40

              30

              20

              10

Zero-Based   0

Notes:

Zero-Based Organization

- *No benchmarking is conducted.*

- *Competitive comparisons are not maintained and used to set stretch targets.*

World-Class Organization

- *Identification and benchmarking of best-in-class processes is encouraged.*

- *Benchmarks are conducted throughout the organization to improve critical work processes.*

✓ Approach   ✓ Deployment   ☐ Results

2.2c   Organization's use of benchmarking for improvement

+ Strengths

    1.

    2.

    3.

– Opportunities for improvement

    1.

    2.

    3.

Strategic planning issues

    Short-term (one to three years)

    1.

    2.

    Long-term (three years or more)

    1.

    2.

2.2d   *Do you evaluate the scope and validity of your benchmark process to improve planning and operational performance?*

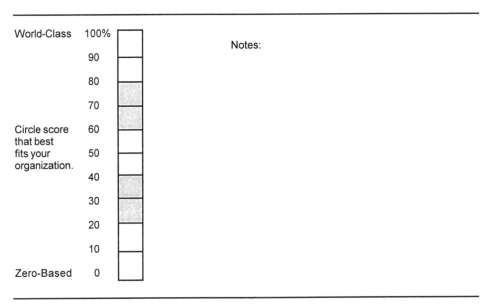

World-Class	100%
	90
	80
	70
Circle score that best fits your organization.	60
	50
	40
	30
	20
	10
Zero-Based	0

Notes:

Zero-Based Organization

- Organization has no documented plan to evaluate and improve the scope, sources, and uses of competitive and benchmark data.

- Organization places no value on competitive benchmarking either inside or outside industry.

World-Class Organization

- Organization's benchmarking program is continuously reviewed for refinement.

- Organization publishes and distributes a document that outlines the benchmark process

☑ Approach   ☑ Deployment   ☐ Results

2.2d   Evaluation and improvement of organization's benchmark process

+ Strengths

   1.

   2.

   3.

– Opportunities for improvement

   1.

   2.

   3.

Strategic planning issues

   Short-term (one to three years)

   1.

   2.

   Long-term (three years or more)

   1.

   2.

2.3 Notes

2.3 Analysis and Uses of Organization-Level Data (40 points)

Describe how data related to quality, customers, and operational performance, together with relevant financial data, are analyzed to support organization-level review, action, and planning.

Areas to Address

a. How customer-related data and results (from category 7.0) are aggregated with other key data and analyses and translated via analysis into useable information to support (1) developing priorities for prompt solutions to customer-related problems and (2) determining key customer-related trends and correlations to support reviews, decision making, and long-term planning.

b. How quality and operational performance data and results (from category 6.0) are aggregated with other key data and analyses and translated via analysis into usable information to support (1) developing priorities for improvements in products/services and organization operations, including cycle time, productivity, and waste reduction and (2) determining key operations-related trends and correlations to support reviews, decision making, and long-term planning.

c. How the organization relates overall improvements in product/service quality and operational performance to changes in overall financial performance to support reviews, decision making, and long-term planning.

d. How the organization evaluates and improves its analysis for use as a key management tool. Include (1) how analysis supports improved data selection and use, (2) how analysis strengthens the integration of overall data use for improved decision making and planning, and (3) how the analysis-access cycle is shortened.

2.3
PERCENT
SCORE

☑ Approach   ☑ Deployment   ☐ Results

2.3a   *Do you systematically analyze all quality data to identify customer trends, problems, and opportunities for improvement (e.g., survey analysis, ROI, and other types of data analysis)?*

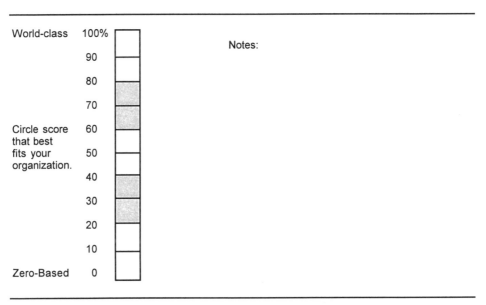

World-class   100%

90

80

70

Circle score   60
that best
fits your   50
organization.
              40

30

20

10

Zero-Based   0

Notes:

Zero-Based Organization	*World-Class Organization*
• *No steps have been taken to shorten the cycle time for data management and data access activities.*	• *Customer survey data are turned into usable information.*
• *Customer data analysis is not systematically linked to key quality indicators established within the organization.*	• *Organization uses quality data to drive improvement.*

☑ Approach   ☑ Deployment   ☐ Results

2.3a   *Customer data analyzed and identified as usable information to*
        support customer satisfaction

+ Strengths

   1.

   2.

   3.

– Opportunities for improvement

   1.

   2.

   3.

Strategic planning issues

   Short-term (one to three years)

   1.

   2.

   Long-term (three years or more)

   1.

   2.

2.3b   *Do you evaluate and improve your data analysis processes? For*
         example, do you look for continuous improvements in the
         organization's approach to short-term improvements within opera-
         tions? How do you improve cycle time, productivity, and waste
         reduction?

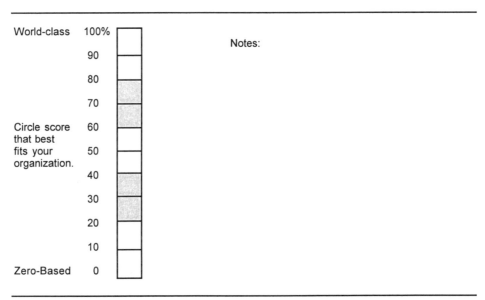

World-class   100%

Notes:

90

80

70

Circle score   60
that best
fits your   50
organization.

40

30

20

10

Zero-Based   0

Zero-Based Organization

- *No evidence that a process exists to ensure that quality-related data are available horizontally and vertically to all levels and functions within the organization.*

- *The data analysis process has not been reviewed for years.*

World-Class Organization

- *Organization has in place a thorough, ongoing search for best-in-class processes.*

- *Organization conducts benchmarks to improve product and service delivery cycle time, reduction of internal processes, supplier performance, and internal operations and performance.*

☑ Approach   ☑ Deployment   ☐ Results

2.3b   *Quality and operational performance data translated into usable
         information to support decision making and planning*

+ Strengths

   1.

   2.

   3.

– Opportunities for improvement

   1.

   2.

   3.

Strategic planning issues

   Short-term (one to three years)

   1.

   2.

   Long-term (three years or more)

   1.

   2.

2.3c   *Does your organization collect key cost, financial, and market data
and translate it into usable information for employees to use to
support decision making and long-term planning?*

World-class   100%

90

80

70

Circle score   60
that best
fits your   50
organization.
40

30

20

10

Zero-Based   0

Notes:

Zero-Based Organization

- *No evidence exists that organization collects key cost, financial and market data and translates them into information for employees to use to improve decision making and long-term planning.*
- *No comparisons are made by organization of its own financial performance against that of its competitors based on key cost, financial, and market data.*

World-Class Organization

- *Cost and financial data are summarized for employees on a monthly and quarterly basis. This data analysis allows organization to maintain the optimal balance of lowest cost with highest response to customer requirements.*
- *Organization makes comparisons among business units showing how quality and operational performance improvement have improved financial performance.*

[✓] Approach   [✓] Deployment   [ ] Results

2.3c Financial and market data translated into usable information to support organization's decision making and long-term planning

+ Strengths

 1.

 2.

 3.

– Opportunities for improvement

 1.

 2.

 3.

Strategic planning issues

 Short-term (one to three years)

 1.

 2.

 Long-term (three years or more)

 1.

 2.

2.3d   *How does your organization shorten access time and improve the*
           internal data you receive?

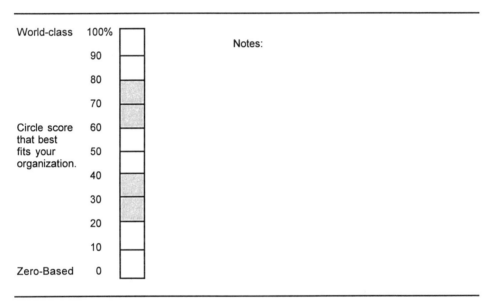

Zero-Based Organization

- *No evidence exists that organi-*
  zation reviews shortened access
  time or improved data analysis.

- *Organization does not use data*
  analysis in decision making.

World-Class Organization

- *Organization reviews and evaluates*
  all data to support and improve
  performance measurement, perfor-
  mance improvement planning, and
  problem identification and resolution.

- *Evaluation of data selection and*
  use is continuously reviewed for
  improvement throughout the
  organization.

✔ Approach   ✔ Deployment   ☐ Results

2.3d   Key indicators used to evaluate and improve data analysis

+ Strengths

  1.

  2.

  3.

– Opportunities for improvement

  1.

  2.

  3.

Strategic planning issues

  Short-term (one to three years)

  1.

  2.

  Long-term (three years or more)

  1.

  2.

Source of the following: 1994 Award Criteria;
Malcolm Baldrige National Quality Award examination
items and notes are excerpted throughout
Measuring Up to the Baldrige.

3.0

Strategic
Quality Planning

Total section value: 60 points

The *Strategic Quality Planning* category examines the organization's planning process and how all key quality requirements are integrated into overall business planning. Also examined are the organization's short- and long-term plans and how quality and performance requirements are deployed to all work units.

3.1 Notes

3.1 Strategic Quality and Organization Performance Planning Process (35 points)

Describe the organization's business planning process for the short term (one to three years) and longer term (three years or more) for customer satisfaction leadership and overall operational performance improvement. Include how this process integrates quality and operational performance requirements and how plans are deployed.

Areas to Address

a. How the organization develops strategies and business plans to address quality and customer satisfaction leadership for the short term and longer term. Describe how plans consider (1) customer requirements and the expected evolution of these requirements; (2) projections of the competitive environment; (3) risks—financial, market, technological, and societal; (4) organization capabilities, such as human resources and research and development, to address key new requirements or market leadership opportunities; and (5) supplier capabilities.
b. How strategies and plans address operational performance improvement. Describe how the following are considered: (1) realigning work processes ("reengineering") to improve customer focus and operational performance and (2) productivity and cycle-time improvement and reduction in waste.
c. How plans are deployed. Describe (1) how the organization deploys plan requirements to work units and to suppliers, and how it ensures alignment of work-unit plans and activities and (2) how resources are committed to meet plan requirements.
d. How the organization evaluates and improves (1) its planning process, (2) deploying plan requirements to work units, and (3) receiving planning input from work units.

☐ **3.1 PERCENT SCORE**

✓ Approach   ✓ Deployment   ☐ Results

3.1a   How is your overall business planning process integrated with individual and departmental planning and goal setting for the short term and the longer term?

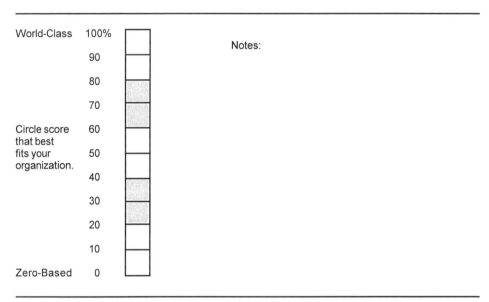

World-Class	100%		Notes:
	90		
	80		
	70		
Circle score that best fits your organization.	60		
	50		
	40		
	30		
	20		
	10		
Zero-Based	0		

Zero-Based Organization

- *No evidence exists that organization develops long-term strategic plans.*

- *Organization does not have a strategic plan in place.*

World-Class Organization

- *Customers are involved in the strategic planning process for both short-term and long-term planning.*

- *Employees at all levels of the organization are involved in both short-term and long-term planning.*

☑ Approach ☑ Deployment ☐ Results

3.1a   Plans and strategies developed for the short term and longer term

+ Strengths

   1.

   2.

   3.

– Opportunities for improvement

   1.

   2.

   3.

Strategic planning issues

   Short-term (one to three years)

   1.

   2.

   Long-term (three years or more)

   1.

   2.

3.1b   Does your organization consider reengineering or realigning core work processes when developing a strategic plan to improve work performance?

World-Class   100%

Notes:

90

80

70

Circle score   60
that best
fits your   50
organization.
40

30

20

10

Zero-Based   0

Zero-Based Organization

- *Appears organization does not include cycle-time improvement and reduction in waste in its strategic planning process.*

- *Organization does not integrate improved cycle time with customer focus and operational performance in its strategic plan.*

World-Class Organization

- *Organization reviews core work processes and addresses cycle-time reduction in its short-term and long-term strategic planning process.*

- *All core work processes are reviewed annually during the strategic planning process to improve customer focus and operational performance.*

☑ Approach   ☑ Deployment   ☐ Results

3.1b   *Strategies and plans in place that address operational performance improvement*

+ Strengths

   1.

   2.

   3.

– Opportunities for improvement

   1.

   2.

   3.

Strategic planning issues

   Short-term (one to three years)

   1.

   2.

   Long-term (three years or more)

   1.

   2.

3.1c   Are your organization's strategic plans deployed throughout your organization?

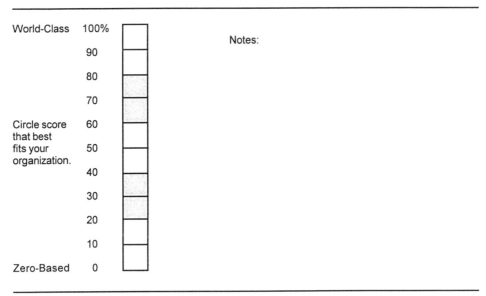

World-Class   100%

Notes:

90

80

70

Circle score   60
that best
fits your   50
organization.
               40

30

20

10

Zero-Based   0

Zero-Based Organization	**World-Class Organization**
• No system exists for data collection.	• Continuous-improvement methods are utilized to improve the scope and quality of data collection throughout the organization.
• No strategic plan in place to prioritize and coordinate data collection throughout the organization.	• Data and information collection are aligned with organization's cycle-time reduction plans and needs.

☑ Approach   ☑ Deployment   ☐ Results

3.1c   Strategic plans deployed throughout the organization

+ Strengths

   1.

   2.

   3.

– Opportunities for improvement

   1.

   2.

   3.

Strategic planning issues

   Short-term (one to three years)

   1.

   2.

   Long-term (three years or more)

   1.

   2.

3.1d   *Is your organization's strategic planning process evaluated and reviewed continuously?*

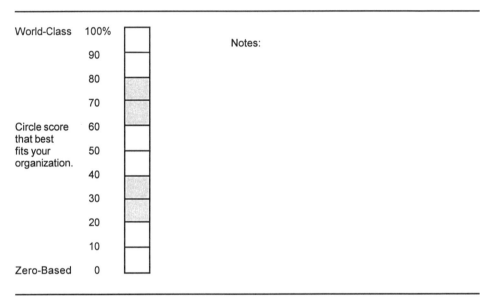

World-Class   100%

Notes:

90

80

70

Circle score   60
that best
fits your   50
organization.

40

30

20

10

Zero-Based   0

Zero-Based Organization

- *Plans bear little or no relation to actions taken by the workforce. Plans are not followed or reviewed by employee groups throughout the organization.*

- *Organization does not evaluate and review strategic plans.*

World-Class Organization

- *Each department reviews plans and gives input to organization's strategic plan.*

- *Each work area has strategic objectives listed and reviews these objectives quarterly.*

☑ Approach   ☑ Deployment   ☐ Results

3.1d   *Strategic plans and goals evaluated and reviewed continuously*

+ Strengths

1.

2.

3.

– Opportunities for improvement

1.

2.

3.

Strategic planning issues

Short-term (one to three years)

1.

2.

Long-term (three years or more)

1.

2.

3.2 Notes

3.2   Quality and Performance Plans (25 points)

Summarize the organization's specific quality and operational performance plans for the short term (one to three years) and the longer term (three years or more).

Areas to Address

a. For planned products, services, and customer markets, summarize (1) key quality requirements to achieve or retain leadership and (2) key organization operational performance requirements.

b. Outline of the organization's deployment of principal short-term quality and operational performance plans. Include (1) a summary of key requirements and associated operational performance measures or indicators deployed to work units and suppliers and (2) a brief description of resources committed for key needs such as capital equipment, facilities, education and training, and new hires.

c. Outline of how principal long-term (three years or more) quality and operational performance requirements (from 3.2a) will be addressed.

d. Two-to-five-year projection of key measures and/or indicators of the organization's quality and operational performance. Describe how quality and operational performance might be expected to compare with key competitors and key benchmarks over this time period. Briefly explain the comparisons, including any estimates or assumptions made regarding the projected quality and operational performance of competitors or changes in benchmarks.

3.2
PERCENT
SCORE

✓ Approach   ✓ Deployment   ☐ Results

109

3.2a   Does your organization have major quality-improvement goals and strategies? List them.

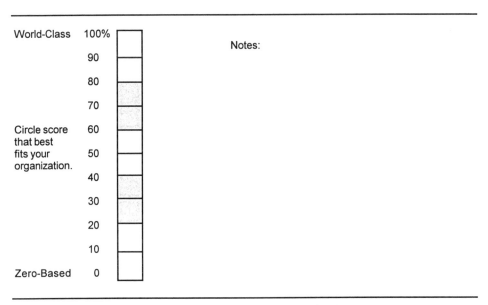

World-Class   100%

Notes:

90

80

70

Circle score   60
that best
fits your   50
organization.

40

30

20

10

Zero-Based   0

Zero-Based Organization

- *No evidence exists that short- and long-term quality goals are established by the organization.*

- *Organization has long-term quality goals established for only one department.*

World-Class Organization

- *Both short- and long-term quality goals are fully integrated into the organization's leadership objectives.*

- *Each department has in place quality-improvement goals and strategies.*

☑ Approach   ☑ Deployment   ☐ Results

3.2a   Major quality and performance goals and strategies

+ Strengths

   1.

   2.

   3.

– Opportunities for improvement

   1.

   2.

   3.

Strategic planning issues

   Short-term (one to three years)

   1.

   2.

   Long-term (three years or more)

   1.

   2.

3.2b   *Summarize your organization's short-term (annual) goals and explain how these goals are deployed to both employees and suppliers.*

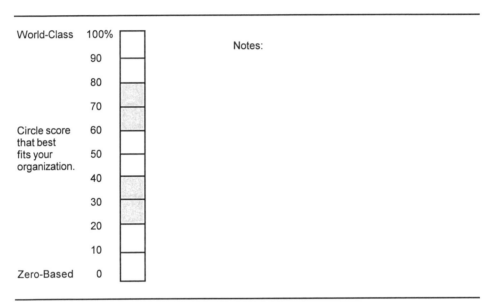

World-Class   100%

90

80

70

Circle score   60
that best
fits your   50
organization.
                40

30

20

10

Zero-Based   0

Notes:

Zero-Based Organization

- *Short-term goals are not shared beyond the senior management level.*

- *Suppliers are not informed of their involvement within the organization's short-term plan.*

World-Class Organization

- *Short-term plans are deployed to individual departments throughout the organization.*

- *Each employee receives a monthly update of organization's progress toward meeting short-term goals.*

☑ Approach   ☑ Deployment   ☐ Results

3.2b   Principal short-term plans and goals

+ Strengths

    1.

    2.

    3.

– Opportunities for improvement

    1.

    2.

    3.

Strategic planning issues

    Short-term (one to three years)

    1.

    2.

    Long-term (three years or more)

    1.

    2.

3.2c   Explain how your organization's long-term goals and requirements relate to improving quality.

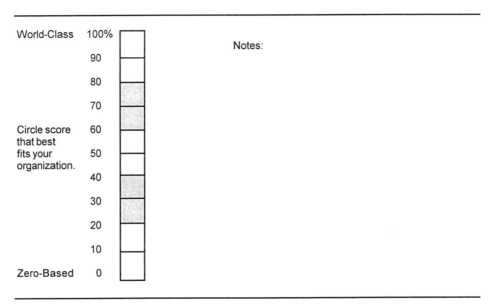

World-Class	100%
	90
	80
	70
Circle score that best fits your organization.	60
	50
	40
	30
	20
	10
Zero-Based	0

Notes:

Zero-Based Organization	*World-Class Organization*
• *Long-term strategic planning target dates are not shared throughout the organization.*	• *Long-term plans are shared with employees at all levels, customers, and suppliers.*
• *No long-term plans in existence.*	• *Long-term goal progress is shared with employees, customers, and suppliers.*

☑ Approach   ☑ Deployment   ☐ Results

3.2c   Principal long-term plans and goals

+ Strengths

   1.

   2.

   3.

− Opportunities for improvement

   1.

   2.

   3.

Strategic planning issues

   Short-term (one to three years)

   1.

   2.

   Long-term (three years or more)

   1.

   2.

3.2d   *What do you project the benefits to be if your organization actually meets the goals outlined in your long- and short-term business plans? How will this compare with your competition and your key benchmarks?*

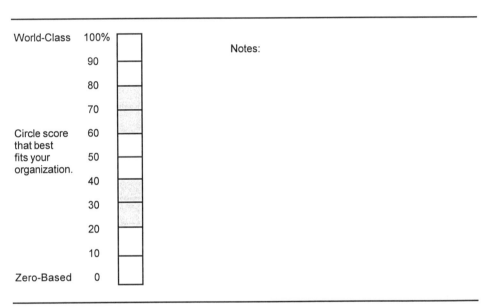

World-Class   100%

90

80

70

Circle score   60
that best
fits your   50
organization.

40

30

20

10

Zero-Based   0

Notes:

Zero-Based Organization	*World-Class Organization*
• *Appears projections are not shared with all employees.*	• *Long-term projections have been developed.*
• *No comparative benchmarks are made by organization.*	• *Long- and short-term projections are made after competitive and benchmark comparisons are made.*

✓ Approach   ✓ Deployment   ☐ Results

3.2d   Projection of changes in quality levels

+ Strengths

    1.

    2.

    3.

– Opportunities for improvement

    1.

    2.

    3.

Strategic planning issues

    Short-term (one to three years)

        1.

        2.

    Long-term (three years or more)

        1.

        2.

Source of the following: 1994 Award Criteria;
Malcolm Baldrige National Quality Award examination
items and notes are excerpted throughout
Measuring Up to the Baldrige.

4.0

Human Resources Development and Management

Total section value: 150 points

The *Human Resources Development and Management* category examines the key elements of how the organization develops and realizes the full potential of the workforce to pursue the organization's quality and performance objectives. Also examined are the organization's efforts to build and maintain an environment for organizational growth.

4.1 Notes

4.1 Human Resources Planning and Management (20 points)

Describe how the organization's overall human resources management, plans, and processes are integrated with its overall quality and operational performance plans and how human resources development and management fully address the needs and development of the entire workforce.

Areas to Address

a. Brief description of the most important human resources plans (derived from category 3.0). Include (1) development, including education, training, and empowerment; (2) mobility, flexibility, and changes in work organization, work processes, or work schedules; (3) reward, recognition, benefits, and compensation; and (4) recruitment, including possible changes in diversity of the workforce. Distinguish between the short term (one to three years) and the longer term (three years or more), as appropriate.

b. How the organization improves key personnel processes. Describe key improvement methods for processes such as recruitment, hiring, personnel actions, and services to employees, including support services to managers and supervisors. Include a description of key performance measures or indicators, including cycle time, and how they are used in improvement.

c. How the organization evaluates and improves its human resources planning and management using all employee-related data. Include (1) how selection, performance, recognition, job analysis, and training are integrated to support improved performance and development of all categories and types of employees and (2) how human resources planning and management are aligned with organizational strategy and plans.

4.1
PERCENT
SCORE

☑ Approach   ☑ Deployment   ☐ Results

121

4.1a *Are your organization's human resources plans driven by the quality goals outlined in your strategic business plan (e.g., training, development, hiring, employee involvement, empowerment, and recognition)?*

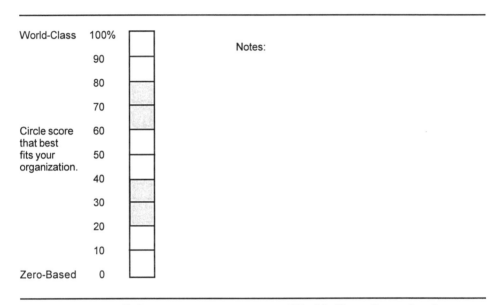

World-Class 100%	Notes:
90	
80	
70	
Circle score 60	
that best	
fits your 50	
organization.	
40	
30	
20	
10	
Zero-Based 0	

Zero-Based Organization	*World-Class Organization*
• *Performance evaluations not written in language to reinforce organization's quality values.*	• *Human resources plans integrated with the organization's strategic plan.*
• *Training widely dispersed but not focused for each employee's indi 'ual career development withi.. the organization.*	• *Organization reflects a team culture and supports this concept through its employee training programs.*

☑ Approach ☑ Deployment ☐ Results

4.1a   Human resources plans

+ Strengths

   1.

   2.

   3.

– Opportunities for improvement

   1.

   2.

   3.

Strategic planning issues

   Short-term (one to three years)

   1.

   2.

   Long-term (three years or more)

   1.

   2.

4.1b   *Are your organization's human resources strategies and goals*
           related to your organization's overall quality improvement goals
           (e.g., hiring, recruitment, personnel actions, employee services)?

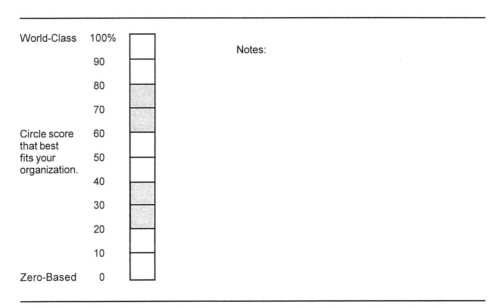

Notes:

Zero-Based Organization

- *No process in place for recruitment and hiring of new employees that is reflective of organization's quality culture.*

- *Organization has a higher-than-industry-average turnover rate.*

World-Class Organization

- *Organization has in place employee teams that focus on improving personnel processes.*

- *Improvement action system in place that allows employee input and ensures management response within a designated time.*

☑ Approach   ☑ Deployment   ☐ Results

4.1b   *Key quality goals for human resources management*

+ Strengths

   1.

   2.

   3.

– Opportunities for improvement

   1.

   2.

   3.

Strategic planning issues

   Short-term (one to three years)

   1.

   2.

   Long-term (three years or more)

   1.

   2.

4.1c   *Give specific examples of how your organization uses employee-related data to improve human resources management (e.g., employee selection process, quality of training, employee development).*

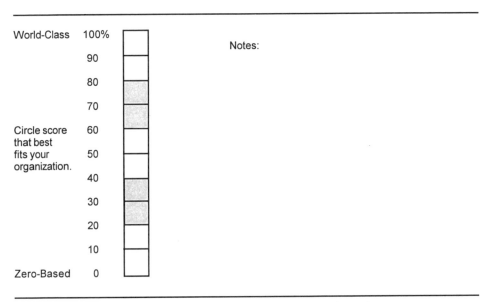

World-Class   100%

90

80

70

Circle score   60
that best
fits your   50
organization.

40

30

20

10

Zero-Based   0

Notes:

Zero-Based Organization	World-Class Organization
• *Human resources management appears not to be driven by employee-related data.*	• *Organization uses an employee satisfaction survey and participative management survey to gauge employee satisfaction.*
• *All improvement within human resources management is anecdotal.*	• *Organization collects data on turnover, absenteeism, safety, grievances, involvement, recognition, training, and employee exit interviews to drive improvement.*

✓ Approach   ✓ Deployment   ☐ Results

4.1c   Analysis and use of data to improve human resources management

+ Strengths

   1.

   2.

   3.

– Opportunities for improvement

   1.

   2.

   3.

Strategic planning issues

   Short-term (one to three years)

     1.

     2.

   Long-term (three years or more)

     1.

     2.

4.2 Notes

4.2 Employee Involvement (40 points)

Describe how all employees are enabled to contribute effectively to meeting the organization's quality and operational performance plans.

Summarize trends in effectiveness and extent of involvement.

Areas to Address

a. How the organization promotes ongoing employee contributions, individually and in groups, to improvement in quality and operational performance. Include how and how quickly the organization gives feedback to contributors.

b. How the organization increases employee empowerment, responsibility, and innovation. Include a brief summary of principal plans for all categories of employees, based upon the most important requirements for each category.

c. How the organization evaluates and improves the effectiveness, extent, and type of involvement of all categories and all types of employees. Include how effectiveness, extent, and types of involvement are linked to key quality and operational performance improvement results.

d. Trends in key measures and/or indicators of the *effectiveness* and *extent* of employee involvement.

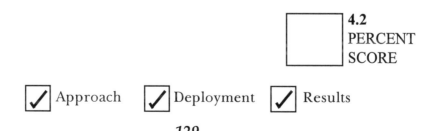

```
┌─────┐ 4.2
│     │ PERCENT
│     │ SCORE
└─────┘
```

☑ Approach   ☑ Deployment   ☑ Results

4.2a   *How does your organization promote employee contributions to quality performance objectives?*

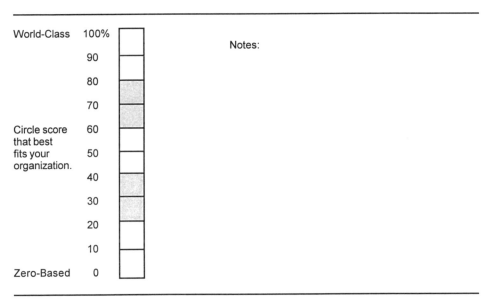

Notes:

Zero-Based Organization	World-Class Organization
• *Employee contributions are not encouraged or acknowledged.*	• *Special recognition awards given to individual employees and employee teams.*
• *Organization promotes contributions made by senior executives.*	• *President's club award in place to promote employee contributions to organization's quality efforts.*

☑ Approach   ☑ Deployment   ☐ Results

4.2a   Trends and practices to promote employee involvement

+ Strengths

    1.

    2.

    3.

– Opportunities for improvement

    1.

    2.

    3.

Strategic planning issues

    Short-term (one to three years)

    1.

    2.

    Long-term (three years or more)

    1.

    2.

4.2b   *Does your organization give all employees the authority or autonomy to solve problems and make decisions within their work areas?*

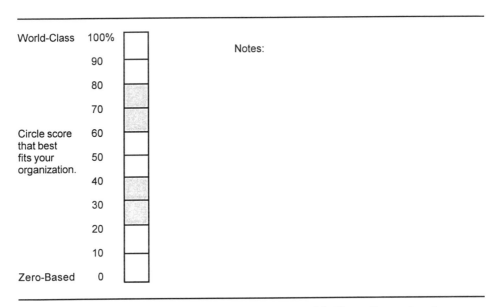

World-Class   100%

               90

               80

               70

Circle score   60
that best
fits your   50
organization.

               40

               30

               20

               10

Zero-Based   0

Notes:

Zero-Based Organization

- *Organization is bureaucratic with a formal structure that does not encourage employee authority or autonomy.*

- *Employees are penalized for being empowered and innovative.*

World-Class Organization

- *Employees at all levels are empowered to make decisions and use innovation within their work areas.*

- *Organization has developed a recognition program that promotes employee empowerment and innovation.*

☑ Approach   ☑ Deployment   ☐ Results

4.2b   Principal goals and trends for employee involvement

+ Strengths

    1.

    2.

    3.

– Opportunities for improvement

    1.

    2.

    3.

Strategic planning issues

    Short-term (one to three years)

    1.

    2.

    Long-term (three years or more)

    1.

    2.

4.2c   *Does your organization evaluate and measure the extent and effectiveness of efforts to increase involvement, empowerment, and innovation?*

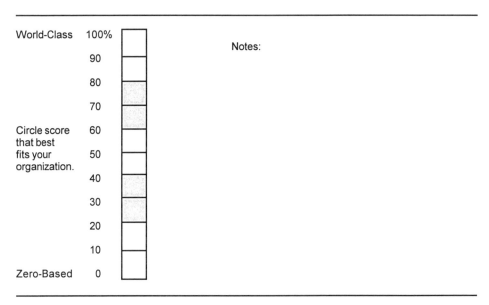

World-Class   100%

90

80

70

Circle score   60
that best
fits your   50
organization.

40

30

20

10

Zero-Based   0

Notes:

Zero-Based Organization	World-Class Organization
• *Lack of formal and informal testing of the organization's climate to determine the degree of employee involvement and satisfaction.*	• *Employee satisfaction results are used to evaluate the extent of employee involvement and to identify impediments to involvement.*
• *Management has no concern for employee involvement and satisfaction.*	• *Employee focus groups are used to evaluate and improve employee involvement throughout organization.*

☑ Approach   ☑ Deployment   ☐ Results

4.2c   _Key indicators used to evaluate the extent and effectiveness of the employee involvement processes_

+ Strengths

    1.

    2.

    3.

– Opportunities for improvement

    1.

    2.

    3.

Strategic planning issues

    Short-term (one to three years)

    1.

    2.

    Long-term (three years or more)

    1.

    2.

4.2d   Does your organization encourage employee involvement at all levels? Are there key measures and/or indicators in place to assess the effectiveness and extent of employee involvement?

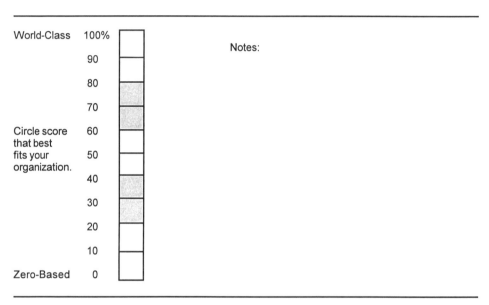

World-Class   100%

90

80

70

Circle score   60
that best
fits your   50
organization.

40

30

20

10

Zero-Based   0

Notes:

Zero-Based Organization

- *No system in place to gauge employee involvement.*

- *Key measures of employee involvement discouraged by senior leaders.*

World-Class Organization

- *Organization encourages, tracks, and measures employee involvement and suggestions systemwide.*

- *Organization has in place key measures to assess employee involvement at all levels.*

☐ Approach   ☐ Deployment   ☑ Results

4.2d   Trends and current levels of involvement by all employees

+ Strengths

　　1.

　　2.

　　3.

– Opportunities for improvement

　　1.

　　2.

　　3.

Strategic planning issues

　　Short-term (one to three years)

　　1.

　　2.

　　Long-term (three years or more)

　　1.

　　2.

4.3 Notes

4.3   Employee Education and Training (40 points)

Describe how the organization determines quality and related education-and-training needs for all employees. Show how this determination addresses organization plans and supports employee growth. Outline how such education and training are evaluated, and summarize key trends in the effectiveness and extent of education and training.

Areas to Address

a. How the organization determines needs for the types and amounts of quality and related education and training for all employees, taking into account their differing needs. Include (1) linkage to short-and long-term plans, including organizationwide access to skills in problem solving, waste reduction, and process simplification; (2) growth and career opportunities for employees; and (3) how employees' input is sought and used in the needs determination.

b. How quality and related education and training are delivered and reinforced. Include (1) description of education-and-training delivery for all categories of employees, (2) on-the-job application of knowledge and skills, and (3) quality-related orientation for new employees.

c. How the organization evaluates and improves its quality and related education and training. Include how the evaluation supports improved needs determination, taking into account (1) relating on-the-job performance improvement to key quality and operational-performance improvement targets and results and (2) growth and progression of all categories and types of employees.

d. Trends in key measures and/or indicators of the *effectiveness* and *extent* of quality and related education and training.

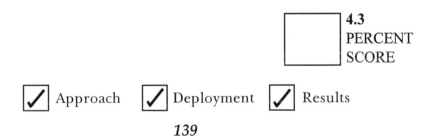

4.3
PERCENT
SCORE

☑ Approach   ☑ Deployment   ☑ Results

139

4.3a   *Does your organization conduct a systematic needs assessment to determine the specific educational needs of different categories of employees?*

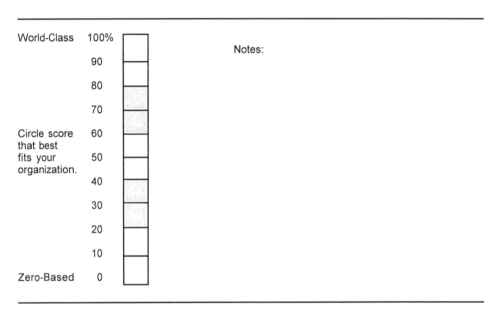

World-Class   100%

90

80

70

Circle score   60
that best
fits your   50
organization.

40

30

20

10

Zero-Based   0

Notes:

Zero-Based Organization

- *No evidence that training needs assessment surveys are being conducted.*

- *Employees' input is not sought or considered when determining training needs.*

World-Class Organization

- *Organization conducts needs assessment surveys periodically.*

- *Training needs are integrated with organization's short- and long-term strategic goals.*

✓ Approach   ✓ Deployment   ☐ Results

4.3a   Key trends assessing quality education and training needs

+ Strengths

   1.

   2.

   3.

– Opportunities for improvement

   1.

   2.

   3.

Strategic planning issues

   Short-term (one to three years)

   1.

   2.

   Long-term (three years or more)

   1.

   2.

4.3b Is quality and related education and training that is received by employees applied and reinforced on-the-job?

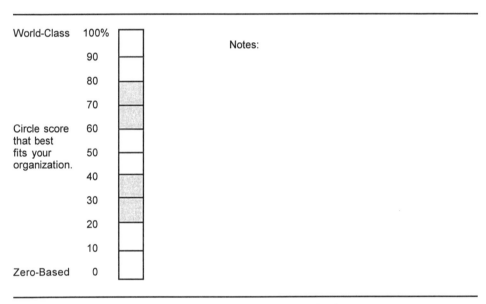

World-Class　100%

90

80

70

Circle score　60
that best
fits your　50
organization.

40

30

20

10

Zero-Based　0

Notes:

Zero-Based Organization

- *No employee training provided.*

- *Organization uses only on-the-job training for employees. No formal training program exists.*

World-Class Organization

- *Training throughout the organization is applied and reinforced on-the-job.*

- *All training throughout the organization is integrated with short-and long-term improvement plans.*

☑ Approach　☑ Deployment　☐ Results

4.3b   *Key trends in quality education and training and on-the-job application*

+ Strengths

    1.

    2.

    3.

– Opportunities for improvement

    1.

    2.

    3.

Strategic planning issues

    Short-term (one to three years)

    1.

    2.

    Long-term (three years or more)

    1.

    2.

4.3c   *What methods and indicators does your organization use to ensure that clear improvements in both employee behavior and quality improvement in the employee's work areas are being demonstrated through improved education and training interventions?*

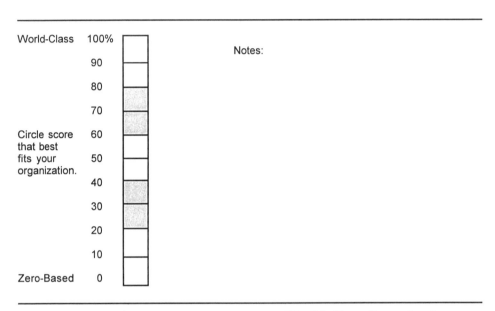

Notes:

Zero-Based Organization	World-Class Organization
• *Lack of training follow-up beyond course evaluation.*	• *After employee training course, questionnaires are distributed to all participants and their managers to gauge behavior and quality improvement within their work areas.*
• *No evidence that most-qualified staff are serving as trainers.*	• *Training is focused and measured against improved job and operational-performance improvement targets and results.*

☑ Approach   ☑ Deployment   ☐ Results

4.3c   Methods and indicators used to evaluate and improve training

+ Strengths

   1.

   2.

   3.

− Opportunities for improvement

   1.

   2.

   3.

Strategic planning issues

   Short-term (one to three years)

   1.

   2.

   Long-term (three years or more)

   1.

   2.

4.3d   *Does your organization measure employee training results by category of employee?*

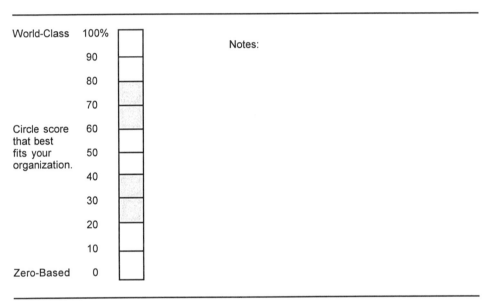

World-Class   100%

Notes:

90

80

70

Circle score that best fits your organization.

60

50

40

30

20

10

Zero-Based   0

Zero-Based Organization	*World-Class Organization*
• *Training results are not measured.*	• *Trend results are segmented by category of employee.*
• *Organization does not segment training results by employee categories.*	• *Training effectiveness is measured among employee groups.*

☐ Approach   ☐ Deployment   ☑ Results

4.3d   Training results measured by employee categories

+ Strengths

1.

2.

3.

– Opportunities for improvement

1.

2.

3.

Strategic planning issues

Short-term (one to three years)

1.

2.

Long-term (three years or more)

1.

2.

4.4 Notes

4.4 Employee Performance and Recognition (25 points)

Describe how the company's approaches to employee performance, recognition, promotion, compensation, reward, and feedback support the improvement of quality and operational performance.

Areas to Address

a. How the company's approaches to employee performance, recognition, promotion, compensation, reward, and feedback for individuals and groups, including managers, support improvement of quality and operational performance. Include (1) how the approaches ensure that quality is reinforced relative to short-term financial considerations and (2) how employees contribute to the company's employee performance and recognition approaches.

b. How the organizationevaluates and improves its employee performance and recognition approaches. Include how the evaluation takes into account (1) effective participation by all categories and types of employees, (2) employee satisfaction information (item 4.5), and (3) key measures or indicators of improved quality and operational performance results.

c. Trends in key measures and/or indicators of the *effectiveness* and *extent* of employee reward and recognition.

4.4
PERCENT
SCORE

☑ Approach   ☑ Deployment   ☑ Results

4.4a   *Does your employee performance, recognition, and reward system support your organization's quality-improvement goals?*

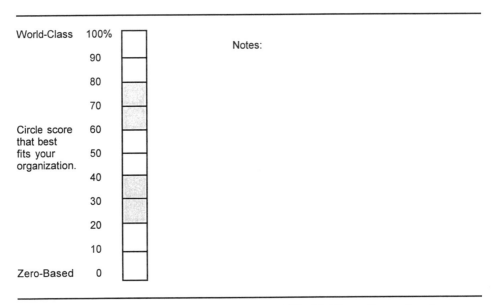

World-Class	100%	
	90	
	80	
	70	
Circle score that best	60	
fits your	50	
organization.		
	40	
	30	
	20	
	10	
Zero-Based	0	

Notes:

Zero-Based Organization	*World-Class Organization*
• *Quality improvement is neither recognized nor rewarded.*	• *Recognition and reward supports organization's quality-improvement goals.*
• *No performance and recognition system is in place.*	• *Organization's performance, recognition, promotion, compensation, reward, and feedback system is integrated with organization's strategic improvement goals.*

✓ Approach   ✓ Deployment   ☐ Results

4.4a   Performance and recognition supporting organizational goals

+ Strengths

   1.

   2.

   3.

– Opportunities for improvement

   1.

   2.

   3.

Strategic planning issues

   Short-term (one to three years)

   1.

   2.

   Long-term (three years or more)

   1.

   2.

4.4b   *Does your organization regularly evaluate and improve the quality of performance measurement, compensation, and recognition programs?*

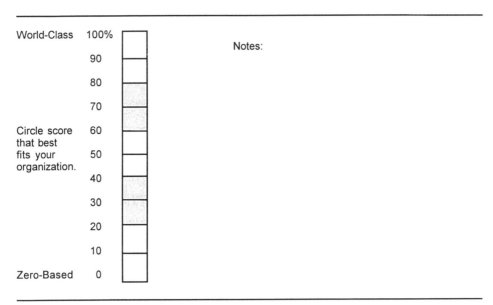

| | Notes: |

Circle score that best fits your organization.

World-Class 100%, 90, 80, 70, 60, 50, 40, 30, 20, 10, Zero-Based 0

Zero-Based Organization

- *No evidence that senior managers use a consistent process to improve their employee recognition programs and that this process is based upon employee input.*

- *Organization does not use key measures of indicators to improve quality and operational performance results.*

World-Class Organization

- *Employee satisfaction survey conducted annually by a third party to gauge improvement in organization's employee performance and recognition approaches.*

- *Employee focus groups, conducted by senior managers to evaluate and improve employee recognition, used to improve performance throughout the organization.*

☑ Approach   ☑ Deployment   ☐ Results

4.4b   Key indicators for organization's performance and recognition

+ Strengths

1.

2.

3.

– Opportunities for improvement

1.

2.

3.

Strategic planning issues

Short-term (one to three years)

1.

2.

Long-term (three years or more)

1.

2.

4.4c   *Does your organization have statistics on the number, percentage, and different types of employees who received recognition awards for quality improvement over the last few years?*

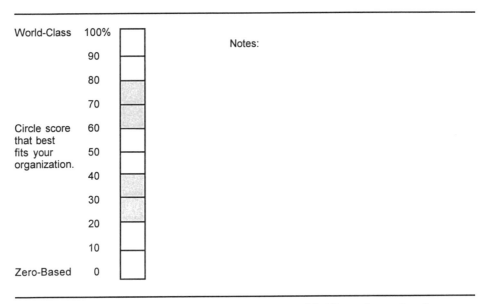

Notes:

Zero-Based Organization	World-Class Organization
• *No recognition system in place.*	• *Steady increase and positive trends in formal and informal recognition given to employees is linked with increased management emphasis on quality improvement.*
• *No trend data collected on employee reward and recognition.*	• *Organization collects data on all employee rewards and recognition.*

☐ Approach   ☐ Deployment   ☑ Results

4.4c   Recognition/reward trends of individuals and groups

+ Strengths

   1.

   2.

   3.

– Opportunities for improvement

   1.

   2.

   3.

Strategic planning issues

   Short-term (one to three years)

     1.

     2.

   Long-term (three years or more)

     1.

     2.

4.5 Notes

4.5 Employee Well-Being and Satisfaction (25 points)

Describe how the organization maintains a work environment conducive to the well-being and growth of all employees.

Summarize trends in key indicators of well-being and satisfaction.

Areas to Address

a. How employee well-being factors such as health, safety, and ergonomics are included in quality-improvement activities. Include principal improvement methods, measures or indicators, and targets for each factor relevant and important to the organization's employee work environment. For accidents and work-related health problems, describe how root causes are determined and how adverse conditions are prevented.

b. What special services, facilities, activities, and opportunities the organization makes available to employees to enhance their work experience and/or to support their overall well-being.

c. How the organization determines employee satisfaction. Include a brief description of methods, frequency, and the specific factors for which satisfaction is determined. Describe how these factors relate to employee motivation and productivity. Segment by employee category or type, as appropriate.

d. Trends in key measures and/or indicators of well-being and satisfaction. Explain important adverse results, if any. For such adverse results, describe how root causes were determined and corrected, and/or give current status. Compare results on the most significant measures or indicators with appropriately selected companies and/or benchmarks.

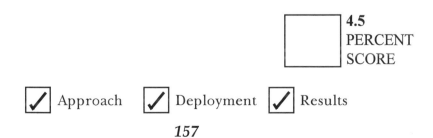

4.5
PERCENT
SCORE

☑ Approach   ☑ Deployment   ☑ Results

157

4.5a   Does your organization constantly work on projects to improve safety, health, ergonomics, employee morale, and job satisfaction?

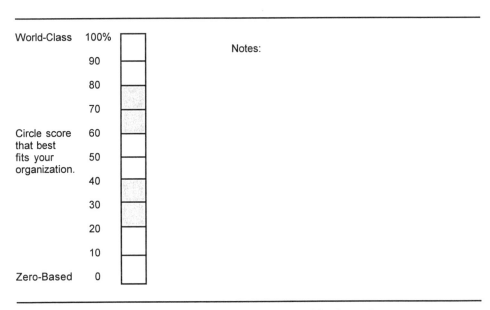

World-Class	100%
	90
	80
	70
Circle score that best fits your organization.	60
	50
	40
	30
	20
	10
Zero-Based	0

Notes:

Zero-Based Organization

- *No specific department or individual dedicated to employee safety.*

- *Senior management not aware of employee morale issues.*

World-Class Organization

- *Employee wellness program in effect.*

- *Employee safety and health issues viewed as paramount in importance to organization.*

☑ Approach   ☑ Deployment   ☐ Results

4.5a   Trends in key indicators of well-being and morale of employees

+ Strengths

   1.

   2.

   3.

– Opportunities for improvement

   1.

   2.

   3.

Strategic planning issues

   Short-term (one to three years)

     1.

     2.

   Long-term (three years or more)

     1.

     2.

4.5b   *Does your organization take a proactive approach in offering special services for employees (e.g., child care facility, ride share, drug rehabilitation program, literacy program)?*

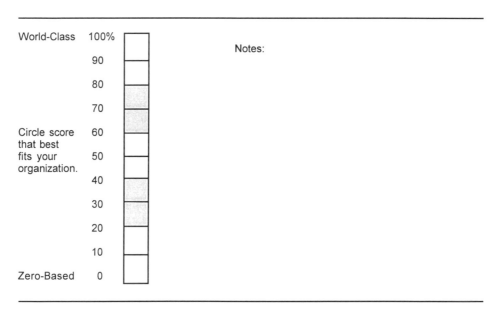

World-Class 100%	Notes:
90	
80	
70	
Circle score 60 that best	
fits your 50 organization.	
40	
30	
20	
10	
Zero-Based 0	

Zero-Based Organization	*World-Class Organization*
• *Not evident to what extent the organization provides special services.*	• *Organization subsidizes child care for employees.*
• *Special services only available for senior managers.*	• *Organization has drug rehabilitation program.*

☑ Approach   ☑ Deployment   ☐ Results

4.5b　　*Special services for employees*

+ Strengths

　　1.

　　2.

　　3.

– Opportunities for improvement

　　1.

　　2.

　　3.

Strategic planning issues

　　Short-term (one to three years)

　　1.

　　2.

　　Long-term (three years or more)

　　1.

　　2.

4.5c   *How does your organization determine employee satisfaction (e.g., surveys, employee focus groups, etc.)?*

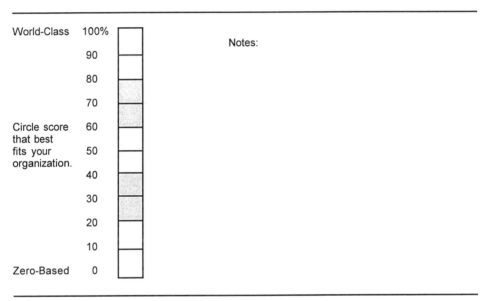

World-Class	100%	
	90	Notes:
	80	
	70	
Circle score that best fits your organization.	60	
	50	
	40	
	30	
	20	
	10	
Zero-Based	0	

Zero-Based Organization

- *Not evident that a process is in place to determine employee satisfaction.*

- *No methods in place to determine employee satisfaction.*

World-Class Organization

- *Annual employee satisfaction survey in place.*

- *Employee focus groups are deployed throughout the organization to discuss and determine employee satisfaction issues.*

☑ Approach   ☑ Deployment   ☐ Results

4.5c   Trend data for determination of employee satisfaction

+ Strengths

   1.

   2.

   3.

− Opportunities for improvement

   1.

   2.

   3.

Strategic planning issues

   Short-term (one to three years)

   1.

   2.

   Long-term (three years or more)

   1.

   2.

*4.5d   Do you have data to support your organization's steady improve-
ment, within your industry, in safety, absenteeism, turnover, attri-
tion rate of customer-contact personnel, employee satisfaction,
grievances, and worker's compensation?*

World-Class   100%

                90
                80
                70
Circle score   60
that best
fits your   50
organization.
                40
                30
                20
                10
Zero-Based   0

Notes:

	Zero-Based Organization	World-Class Organization

Zero-Based Organization

- *No benchmarks are conducted to compare organization's employee satisfaction with that of competition.*

- *Employee well-being not a driving force in organization's strategic plan.*

World-Class Organization

- *Employee well-being and morale is integrated into organization's quality process.*

- *Benchmark data is used for comparison in determining improved employee morale.*

☐ Approach   ☐ Deployment   ☑ Results

4.5d   Data used as key indicators of employee morale

+ Strengths

1.

2.

3.

– Opportunities for improvement

1.

2.

3.

Strategic planning issues

Short-term (one to three years)

1.

2.

Long-term (three years or more)

1.

2.

Source of the following: 1994 Award Criteria;
Malcolm Baldrige National Quality Award examination
items and notes are excerpted throughout
Measuring Up to the Baldrige.

5.0

Management of Process Quality

Total section value: 140 points

The *Management of Process Quality* category examines the systematic processes the organization uses to pursue ever-higher quality and organizational performance. Examined are the key elements of process management, including design, management of process quality for all work units and suppliers, systematic quality improvement, and quality assessment.

5.1 Notes

5.1 Design and Introduction of Quality Products and Services (40 points)

Describe how new and/or modified products and services are designed and introduced and how key production/delivery processes are designed to meet both key product and service quality requirements and organization operational performance requirements.

Areas to Address

a. How products, services, and production/delivery processes are designed. Describe (1) how customer requirements are translated into product and service design requirements; (2) how product and service design requirements, together with the company's operational performance requirements, are translated into production/delivery processes, including an appropriate measurement plan; (3) how all product and service quality requirements are addressed early in the overall design process by appropriate organization units; and (4) how designs are coordinated and integrated to include all phases of production and delivery.

b. How product, service, and production/delivery process designs are reviewed and validated, taking into account as key factors (1) overall product and service performance, (2) process capability and future requirements, and (3) supplier capability and future requirements.

c. How designs and design processes are evaluated and improved so that new product and service introductions and product and service modifications progressively improve in quality and cycle time.

☐ **5.1 PERCENT SCORE**

☑ Approach   ☑ Deployment   ☐ Results

169

5.1a   *Does your organization employ a systematic approach to gathering information about customers' requirements and desires, and then translate that information into product or service characteristics and standards?*

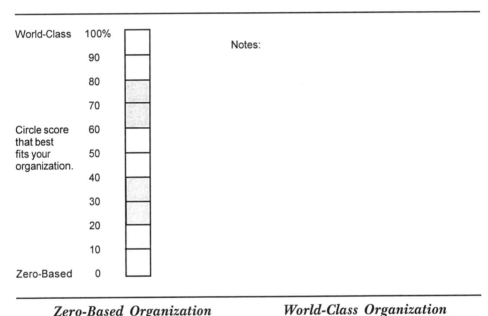

World-Class 100%	Notes:
90	
80	
70	
Circle score 60	
that best	
fits your 50	
organization.	
40	
30	
20	
10	
Zero-Based 0	

Zero-Based Organization	*World-Class Organization*
• *No process in place to determine customer requirements.*	• *Customer surveys used to determine customer requirements.*
• *Design of products and services is not based on customer requirements.*	• *Customer focus groups conducted with all customer levels.*

✓ Approach   ✓ Deployment   ☐ Results

5.1a   From customer requirements to design requirements

\+ Strengths

   1.

   2.

   3.

– Opportunities for improvement

   1.

   2.

   3.

Strategic planning issues

   Short-term (one to three years)

   1.

   2.

   Long-term (three years or more)

   1.

   2.

*5.1b   Describe the overall process your organization uses to design and
         test new products and services.*

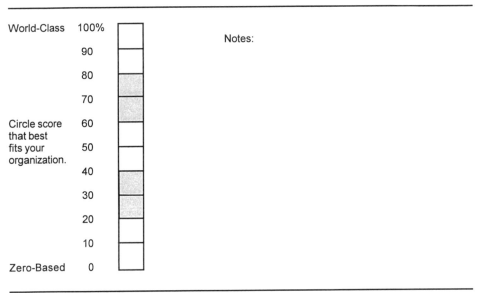

World-Class   100%

                90

                80

                70

Circle score   60
that best
fits your   50
organization.
                40

                30

                20

                10

Zero-Based   0

Notes:

Zero-Based Organization

- *No system in place to design
  and test new products and
  services.*

- *No refined, documented
  research approach in all areas
  to ensure consistent quality in
  design plans and testing before
  introduction of new products
  and services.*

World-Class Organization

- *Documented product and service
  design qualifications and release
  procedures in place to test new
  products and services.*

- *All designs are reviewed and
  validated.*

☑ Approach   ☑ Deployment   ☐ Results

5.1b   Review and validation of design

+ Strengths

    1.

    2.

    3.

– Opportunities for improvement

    1.

    2.

    3.

Strategic planning issues

    Short-term (one to three years)

    1.

    2.

    Long-term (three years or more)

    1.

    2.

5.1c *Does your organization systematically evaluate and shorten design processes for new products or services?*

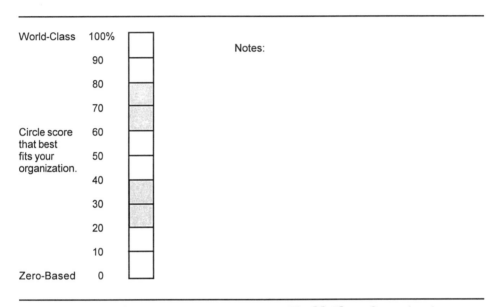

World-Class   100%

Notes:

90

80

70

Circle score   60
that best
fits your   50
organization.

40

30

20

10

Zero-Based   0

Zero-Based Organization

- *No documented procedure for cycle-time reduction in place.*

- *Product and service designs and design processes are not evaluated for improvement.*

World-Class Organization

- *Pilots are used for cycle-time reduction.*

- *System in place to reduce introduction time for new products or services.*

☑ Approach   ☑ Deployment   ☐ Results

5.1c   Evaluation and improvement of designs and design processes

+ Strengths

    1.

    2.

    3.

– Opportunities for improvement

    1.

    2.

    3.

Strategic planning issues

    Short-term (one to three years)

    1.

    2.

    Long-term (three years or more)

    1.

    2.

5.2 Notes

5.2 Process Management: Product and Service Production and Delivery Processes (35 points)

Describe how the organization's key product and service production/ delivery processes are managed to ensure that design requirements are met and that both quality and operational performance are continuously improved.

Areas to Address

a. How the organization maintains the quality and operational performance of the production/delivery processes described in item 5.1. Describe (1) the key processes, their requirements, and how quality and operational performance are tracked and maintained. Include types and frequencies of in-process and end-of-process measurements used; (2) for significant (out-of-control) variations in processes or outputs, how root causes are determined; and (3) how such corrections of variation are made, verified, and integrated into process management.

b. How processes are improved to achieve better quality, cycle time, and operational performance. Describe how each of the following is used or considered: (1) process analysis/simplification, (2) benchmarking information, (3) process research and testing, (4) use of alternative technology, (5) information from customers of the processes—within and outside the organization, and (6) stretch targets.

5.2
PERCENT
SCORE

☑ Approach ☑ Deployment ☐ Results

5.2a   *Does your organization control the processes, and control variations in the processes, used to produce and deliver your products and services?*

World-Class   100%

90

80

70

Circle score   60
that best
fits your   50
organization.

40

30

20

10

Zero-Based   0

Notes:

Zero-Based Organization

- *No integrated product or service control processes exist.*

- *Limited deployment of internal audit, input/output check of products produced, and/or services provided.*

World-Class Organization

- *Rigorous and systematic process for sampling output and ensuring adherence to design plans.*

- *Use of control charts throughout the organization is evident.*

☑ Approach   ☑ Deployment   ☐ Results

5.2a   Process-control assurance

+ Strengths

   1.

   2.

   3.

– Opportunities for improvement

   1.

   2.

   3.

Strategic planning issues

   Short-term (one to three years)

   1.

   2.

   Long-term (three years or more)

   1.

   2.

5.2b   Does your organization use a systematic, planned, and structured evaluation process that ensures better quality, cycle time, and operational performance?

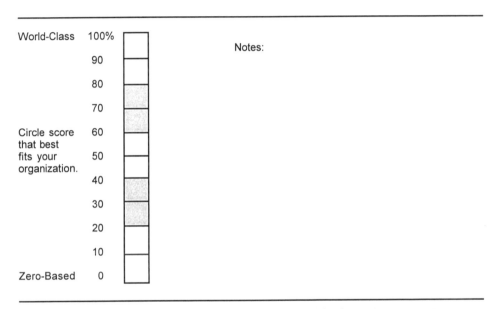

World-Class   100%

90

80

70

Circle score   60
that best
fits your   50
organization.
               40

30

20

10

Zero-Based   0

Notes:

Zero-Based Organization

- *Organization is bureaucratic with a formal structure that does not encourage employee authority or autonomy.*

- *Employees are penalized for being empowered and innovative.*

World-Class Organization

- *Employees at all levels are empowered to make decisions and use innovation within their work areas.*

- *Organization has developed a recognition program that promotes employee empowerment and innovation.*

☑ Approach   ☑ Deployment   ☐ Results

5.2b   *Integration of process improvement into better quality, cycle time,*
        and operational performance

+ Strengths

    1.

    2.

    3.

– Opportunities for improvement

    1.

    2.

    3.

Strategic planning issues

    Short-term (one to three years)

    1.

    2.

    Long-term (three years or more)

    1.

    2.

5.3 Notes

5.3 Process Management: Business and Support Service Processes (30 points)

Describe how the organization's key business and support service processes are designed and managed so that current requirements are met and that quality and operational performance are continuously improved.

Areas to Address

a. How key business and support service processes are designed. Include (1) how key quality and operational performance requirements for business and support services are determined or set and (2) how these quality and operational performance requirements are translated into delivery processes, including an appropriate measurement plan.

b. How the organization maintains the quality and operational performance of business and support service delivery processes. Describe (1) the key processes, their requirements, and how quality and operational performance are tracked and maintained, including types and frequencies of in-process and end-of-process measurements used; (2) for significant (out-of-control) variations in processes or outputs, how root causes are determined; and (3) how corrections of variation are made, verified, and integrated into process management.

c. How processes are improved to achieve better quality, cycle time, and overall operational performance. Describe how each of the following is used or considered: (1) process analysis/simplification, (2) bench-marking information, (3) process research and testing, (4) use of alternative technology, (5) information from customers of the business processes and support services—within and outside the organization, and (6) stretch targets.

☐ 5.3 PERCENT SCORE

☑ Approach ☑ Deployment ☐ Results

183

5.3a   How does your organization handle quality control of your daily business processes and support services?

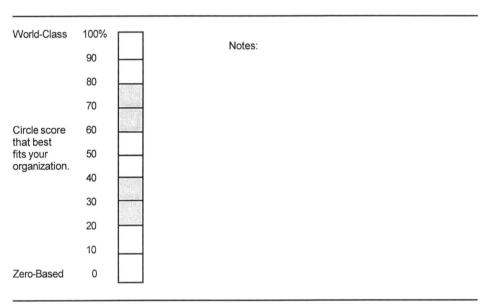

World-Class	100%	
	90	
	80	
	70	
Circle score that best fits your organization.	60	
	50	
	40	
	30	
	20	
	10	
Zero-Based	0	

Notes:

Zero-Based Organization

- *Business processes and support services are not measured.*

- *No root-cause determination is conducted for out-of-control processes in the organization's support areas.*

World-Class Organization

- *Business processes and support services have documented processes.*

- *Out-of-control processes are analyzed by teams using a standardized problem solving process.*

☑ Approach   ☑ Deployment   ☐ Results

5.3a   Maintenance of business processes and support services

+ Strengths

   1.

   2.

   3.

− Opportunities for improvement

   1.

   2.

   3.

Strategic planning issues

   Short-term (one to three years)

   1.

   2.

   Long-term (three years or more)

   1.

   2.

5.3b   Does your organization identify, track, and maintain measurement indicators on key business and support processes (e.g., software services, sales, marketing, public relations, purchasing, legal services, basic research and development, and secretarial and other administrative services)?

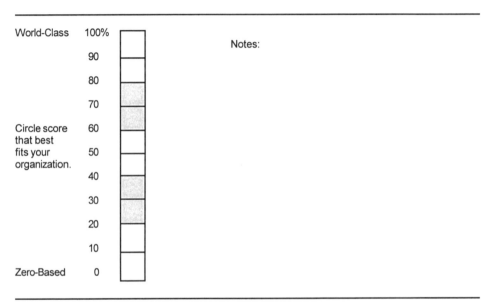

World-Class   100%

90

80

70

Circle score   60
that best
fits your   50
organization.

40

30

20

10

Zero-Based   0

Notes:

Zero-Based Organization

- *Organization is bureaucratic with a formal structure that does not encourage employee authority or autonomy.*

- *Employees are penalized for being empowered and innovative.*

World-Class Organization

- *Employees at all levels are empowered to make decisions and use innovation within their work areas.*

- *Organization has developed a recognition program that promotes employee empowerment and innovation.*

☑ Approach   ☑ Deployment   ☐ Results

5.3b   Organization tracking and maintenance of key business and support processes

+ Strengths

  1.

  2.

  3.

– Opportunities for improvement

  1.

  2.

  3.

Strategic planning issues

  Short-term (one to three years)

  1.

  2.

  Long-term (three years or more)

  1.

  2.

5.3c   *How does your organization identify opportunities for continuous process improvement (e.g., use of competitor benchmark data, systematic analysis of changing market, etc.)?*

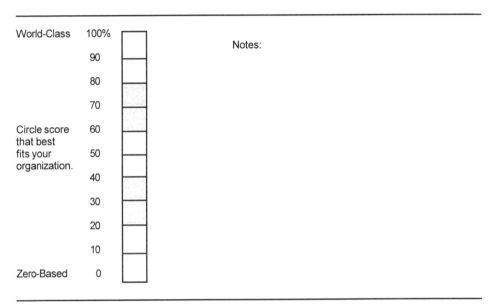

World-Class   100%
                90   Notes:
                80
                70
Circle score   60
that best
fits your   50
organization.
                40
                30
                20
                10
Zero-Based   0

Zero-Based Organization	World-Class Organization
• *No method for verifying that process improvements are made.*	• *Organization regularly conducts benchmarks to identify opportunities for continuous improvement.*
• *Simplification of processes and shortened cycle time within business and support-service areas are not considered by the organization.*	• *Customers are surveyed inside and outside the organization regarding methods to shorten cycle time within business processes and support services.*

✓ Approach   ✓ Deployment   ☐ Results

5.3c   Process improvement to achieve better quality

+ Strengths

1.

2.

3.

– Opportunities for improvement

1.

2.

3.

Strategic planning issues

Short-term (one to three years)

1.

2.

Long-term (three years or more)

1.

2.

5.4 Notes

5.4 Supplier Quality (20 points)

Describe how the company ensures the quality of materials, components, and services furnished by other businesses. Describe also the company's actions and plans to improve supplier quality.

Areas to Address

a. How the organization's quality requirements are defined and communicated to suppliers. Include a brief summary of the principal quality requirements for key suppliers. Also give the measures and/or indicators and expected performance levels for the principal requirements.

b. How the organization determines whether or not its quality requirements are met by suppliers. Describe how performance information is fed back to suppliers.

c. How the organization evaluates and improves its own procurement processes. Include what feedback is sought from suppliers, and how it is used in improvement.

d. Current actions and plans to improve suppliers' abilities to meet key quality, response-time, or other requirements. Include actions and/or plans to minimize inspection, test, audit, or other approaches that might incur unnecessary costs.

5.4
PERCENT
SCORE

☑ Approach   ☑ Deployment   ☐ Results

*5.4a   Does your organization communicate specific quality requirements
          to your most critical suppliers?*

World-Class   100%

                90

Notes:

                80

                70

Circle score   60
that best
fits your   50
organization.

                40

                30

                20

                10

Zero-Based   0

Zero-Based Organization

- *No system in place for supplier partnership or supplier certification.*

- *Organization does not consider supplier performance to be a major hindrance and does not define its requirements to suppliers.*

World-Class Organization

- *Organization has formal supplier certification process in place.*

- *Organization has published quality requirements for all critical suppliers.*

☑ Approach   ☑ Deployment   ☐ Results

5.4a   Communication of requirements to suppliers

+ Strengths

   1.

   2.

   3.

– Opportunities for improvement

   1.

   2.

   3.

Strategic planning issues

   Short-term (one to three years)

   1.

   2.

   Long-term (three years or more)

   1.

   2.

5.4b   *Does your organization have a well-defined process that ensures supplier quality?*

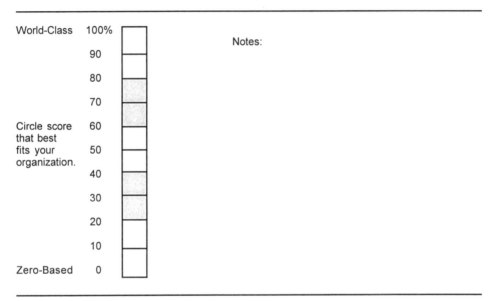

World-Class   100%

90

80

70

Circle score   60
that best
fits your   50
organization.

40

30

20

10

Zero-Based   0

Notes:

Zero-Based Organization

- *Organization has no process in place to ensure quality requirements are met by suppliers.*

- *No supplier feedback mechanism is in place to help organization determine if requirements are met.*

World-Class Organization

- *Formal process exists that ensures quality standards are met by suppliers.*

- *A formal supplier "report card" system is in place to feed back performance information to suppliers.*

☑ Approach   ☑ Deployment   ☐ Results

5.4b   Methods used to ensure supplier quality

+ Strengths

   1.

   2.

   3.

– Opportunities for improvement

   1.

   2.

   3.

Strategic planning issues

   Short-term (one to three years)

   1.

   2.

   Long-term (three years or more)

   1.

   2.

5.4c   *Does your organization evaluate and improve its procurement processes?*

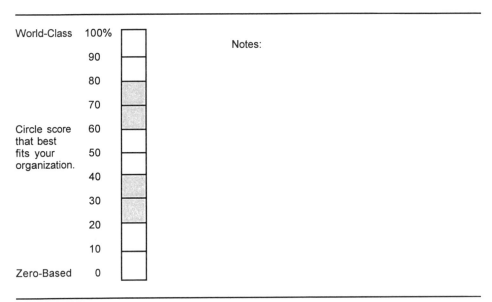

Notes:

Zero-Based Organization	World-Class Organization
• Organization considers its procurement process to be the best and does no evaluation.	• Organization reevaluates procurement processes semi-annually.
• Organization does not consider suppliers as partners in quality improvement.	• Productivity and waste reduction within procurement processes are reviewed by an employee-supplier team quarterly.

☑ Approach   ☑ Deployment   ☐ Results

5.4c   Evaluation and improvement of procurement process

+ Strengths

   1.

   2.

   3.

– Opportunities for improvement

   1.

   2.

   3.

Strategic planning issues

   Short-term (one to three years)

   1.

   2.

   Long-term (three years or more)

   1.

   2.

5.4d   *Has your organization established a cooperative relationship with key suppliers (e.g., supplier partnerships, supplier award program, supplier certification)?*

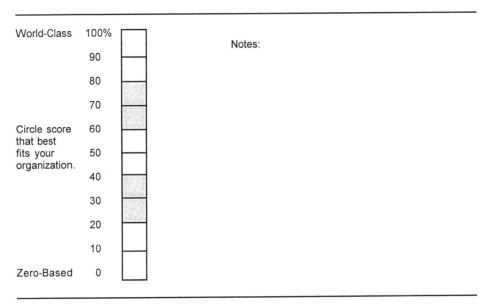

World-Class	100%
	90
	80
	70
Circle score that best fits your organization.	60
	50
	40
	30
	20
	10
Zero-Based	0

Notes:

Zero-Based Organization

- *No system for communicating organization's quality requirements to major suppliers.*

- *No partnerships exist with critical suppliers.*

World-Class Organization

- *Organization has a supplier award/recognition system in place.*

- *Certified-supplier program in place.*

☑ Approach   ☑ Deployment   ☐ Results

5.4d   Strategies/actions to improve supplier quality and responsiveness

+ Strengths

   1.

   2.

   3.

– Opportunities for improvement

   1.

   2.

   3.

Strategic planning issues

   Short-term (one to three years)

   1.

   2.

   Long-term (three years or more)

   1.

   2.

5.5 Notes

5.5 Quality Assessment (15 points)

Describe how the organization assesses the quality and performance of its systems and processes and the quality of its products and services.

Areas to Address

a. How the organization assesses (1) systems and processes and (2) products and services. For (1) and (2), describe (a) what is assessed, (b) how often assessments are made and by whom, and (c) how measurement quality and adequacy of documentation of processes are assured.

b. How assessment findings are used to improve products and services, systems, processes, supplier requirements, and the assessment processes. Include how the organization verifies that assessment findings are acted upon and that the actions are effective.

	5.5 PERCENT SCORE

☑ Approach   ☑ Deployment   ☐ Results

*5.5a   Does your organization audit or assess products, services, and the
systems and processes used to create them?*

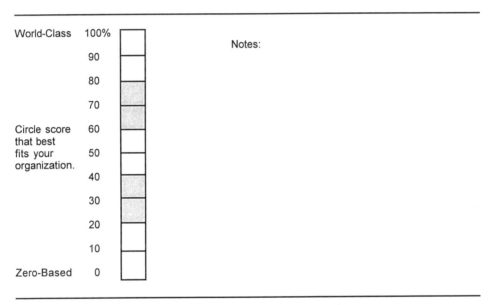

World-Class   100%

Notes:

90

80

70

Circle score   60
that best
fits your   50
organization.
40

30

20

10

Zero-Based   0

Zero-Based Organization

- *No mature audit process in place.*

- *No evidence that process is in place for making documentation readily accessible to those responsible for design, implementation, assessment, and improvement of processes and quality.*

World-Class Organization

- *Products and services are assessed by the use of customer surveys, complaint feedback, warranty data, and market share information.*

- *Organization conducts a quarterly assessment of critical systems and processes used to produce core products/services.*

✓ Approach   ✓ Deployment   ☐ Results

5.5a   *Approaches to assessing systems and processes used in producing quality products/services*

+ Strengths

    1.

    2.

    3.

– Opportunities for improvement

    1.

    2.

    3.

Strategic planning issues

    Short-term (one to three years)

    1.

    2.

    Long-term (three years or more)

    1.

    2.

*5.5b   Does your organization systematically follow up on its assessment
          and correct the problems detected?*

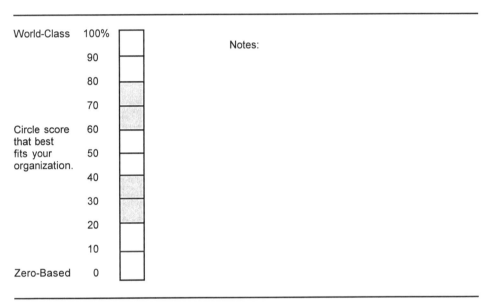

World-Class   100%

Notes:

Circle score
that best
fits your
organization.

Zero-Based   0

Zero-Based Organization

- *No evidence that process assessments are conducted.*

- *Organization does assessments on
  systems and processes only when
  out-of-control process problems
  occur.*

World-Class Organization

- *Assessment findings are deployed to
  teams throughout the organization
  to drive continuous improvement.*

- *All assessment findings are assigned
  a timeline to ensure that progress
  toward improvement is acted upon.*

✓ Approach   ✓ Deployment   ☐ Results

5.5b   *Use of assessment findings to improve systems, processes, and products/services*

+ Strengths

   1.

   2.

   3.

– Opportunities for improvement

   1.

   2.

   3.

Strategic planning issues

   Short-term (one to three years)

   1.

   2.

   Long-term (three years or more)

   1.

   2.

Source of the following: 1994 Award Criteria;
Malcolm Baldrige National Quality Award examination
items and notes are excerpted throughout
Measuring Up to the Baldrige.

6.0

Quality and Operational Results

Total section value: 180 points

The *Quality and Operational Results* category examines the organization's quality levels and improvement trends in quality, organization operational performance, and supplier quality. Also examined are current quality and performance levels relative to those of competitors.

6.1 Notes

6.1 Product and Service Quality Results (70 points)

Summarize trends and current quality levels for key product and service features. Compare current levels with those of competitors and/or appropriate benchmarks.

Areas to Address

a. Trends and current levels for the key measures and/or indicators of product and service quality.

b. Comparisons of current quality levels with that of principal competitors in the organization's key markets, industry averages, industry leaders, and appropriate benchmarks.

6.1
PERCENT
SCORE

☐ Approach   ☐ Deployment   ☑ Results

6.1a   *Does your organization have two years or more of data related to quality improvement of your products and services (e.g., graphs, historical data showing improvement trends, etc.)?*

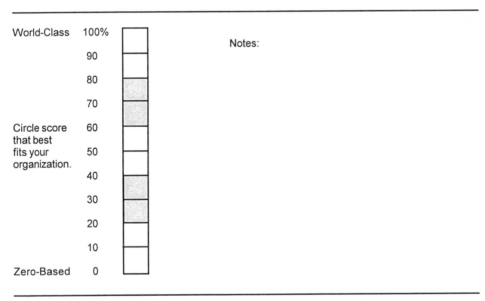

World-Class	100%
	90
	80
	70
Circle score that best fits your organization.	60
	50
	40
	30
	20
	10
Zero-Based	0

Notes:

Zero-Based Organization

- *Not evident that organization is tracking product/service quality during production and after delivery.*

- *Limited tracking of product or service quality.*

World-Class Organization

- *Organization tracks product/ service quality during production and after delivery.*

- *Product/service quality shows positive trends over the past three years.*

☐ Approach   ☐ Deployment   ☑ Results

6.1a   *Trends and current levels for key measures of product and service quality*

+ Strengths

    1.

    2.

    3.

– Opportunities for improvement

    1.

    2.

    3.

Strategic planning issues

    Short-term (one to three years)

    1.

    2.

    Long-term (three years or more)

    1.

    2.

6.1b   *Specifically, how does your organization compare your quality results with those of your competitors?*

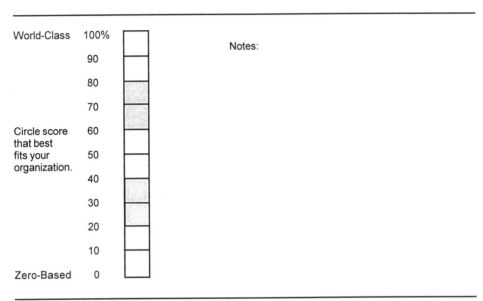

World-Class   100%

90

80

70

Circle score   60
that best
fits your   50
organization.

40

30

20

10

Zero-Based   0

Notes:

Zero-Based Organization

- *No formal benchmarking conducted.*

- *No consistent access to competitive data. Data collected are anecdotal.*

World-Class Organization

- *Organization conducts competitive benchmarks to compare quality results.*

- *Personnel assigned to collect industry/competitor data.*

☐ Approach   ☐ Deployment   ☑ Results

6.1b   *Organization's current quality level comparisons against principal competitors*

+ Strengths

   1.

   2.

   3.

– Opportunities for improvement

   1.

   2.

   3.

Strategic planning issues

   Short-term (one to three years)

   1.

   2.

   Long-term (three years or more)

   1.

   2.

6.2 Notes

6.2 Organization Operational Results (50 points)

Summarize trends and levels in overall organization operational performance. Provide a comparison with competitors and/or appropriate benchmarks.

Areas to Address

a. Trends and current levels for key measures and/or indicators of organization operational performance.

b. Comparison of performance with that of competitors, industry averages, industry leaders, and key benchmarks.

6.2
PERCENT
SCORE

☐ Approach   ☐ Deployment   ☑ Results

6.2a   *Does your organization collect data that measures its operational*
performance (e.g., productivity indices, waste reduction, cycle-time
reduction, environmental improvement)?

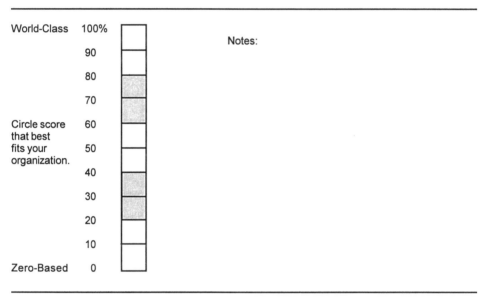

World-Class   100%

Notes:

90

80

70

Circle score   60
that best
fits your   50
organization.
40

30

20

10

Zero-Based   0

Zero-Based Organization	*World-Class Organization*
• *Organization does not collect data on operational performance.*	• *Organization's business plan provides direction (goals and guidance on collecting data) to drive continuous improvement in operations.*
• *Organization has no measures in place for overall organization performance.*	• *Trends have been charted over the past three years and that information deployed throughout the organization.*

☐ Approach   ☐ Deployment   ☑ Results

6.2a   Trends and current levels of organization's operational performance

+ Strengths

   1.

   2.

   3.

– Opportunities for improvement

   1.

   2.

   3.

Strategic planning issues

   Short-term (one to three years)

   1.

   2.

   Long-term (three years or more)

   1.

   2.

6.2b   *How does your organization's data compare with those of competitors and key benchmarks?*

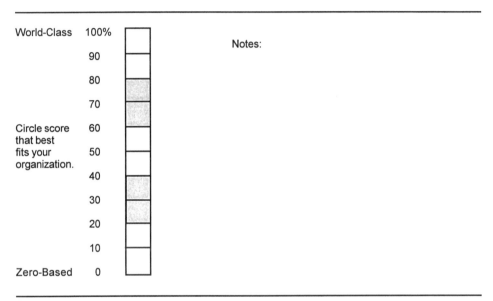

World-Class   100%

90

80

70

Circle score   60
that best
fits your   50
organization.
40

30

20

10

Zero-Based   0

Notes:

Zero-Based Organization

- *Performance measurement data not collected on competitors and industry leaders.*

- *No data comparisons made against key benchmarks.*

World-Class Organization

- *Organization collects benchmark data on industry and world leaders.*

- *Organization collects data against competition and key benchmarks on improvements in product/service design and production/delivery processes.*

☐ Approach   ☐ Deployment   ☑ Results

6.2b   Organization's comparative data on competitors and key benchmarks

+ Strengths

   1.

   2.

   3.

– Opportunities for improvement

   1.

   2.

   3.

Strategic planning issues

   Short-term (one to three years)

   1.

   2.

   Long-term (three years or more)

   1.

   2.

6.3 Notes

6.3 Business and Support Service Results (25 points)

Summarize trends and current levels in quality and operational performance improvement for business processes and support services. Compare results with competitors and/or appropriate benchmarks.

Areas to Address

a. Trends and current levels for key measures and/or indicators of quality and operational performance of business processes and support services.

b. Comparison of performance with appropriately selected companies and benchmarks.

	6.3
	PERCENT
	SCORE

☐ Approach ☐ Deployment ☑ Results

6.3a   Specifically, what data does your organization collect that is related to quality improvement within your business processes and support services?

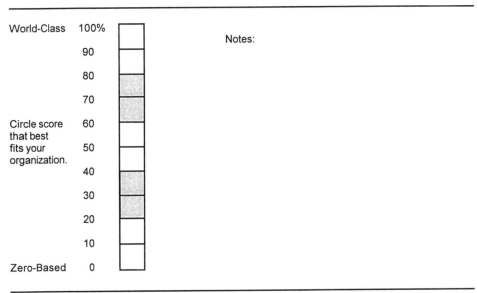

World-Class   100%

90

80

70

Circle score   60
that best
fits your   50
organization.

40

30

20

10

Zero-Based   0

Notes:

Zero-Based Organization

- No quality improvement data analyzed in the business-process and support-service areas.

- Data collection from key business processes and support services are not integrated with organization's strategic operational plan.

World-Class Organization

- All business processes and support services have annual quality improvement objectives for data collection.

- Key measures are collected on cycle time and cost reduction within core business processes and support services.

☐ Approach   ☐ Deployment   ☑ Results

6.3a   Trends and current levels of business processes and support services

+ Strengths

   1.

   2.

   3.

– Opportunities for improvement

   1.

   2.

   3.

Strategic planning issues

   Short-term (one to three years)

   1.

   2.

   Long-term (three years or more)

   1.

   2.

6.3b   Do competitive comparisons demonstrate that your organization is better than industry and world leaders?

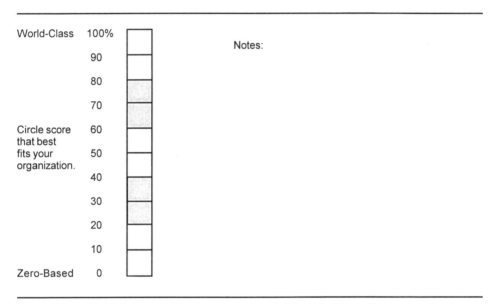

Notes:

World-Class   100%

90

80

70

Circle score   60
that best
fits your   50
organization.
40

30

20

10

Zero-Based   0

Zero-Based Organization

- *Organization does not benchmark industry and world leaders.*

- *Performance data not shared within industry.*

World-Class Organization

- *Organization benchmarks best-in-class processes to compare performance.*

- *Organization uses comparative and benchmark data to gauge performance, regardless of industry.*

☐ Approach   ☐ Deployment   ☑ Results

6.3b   Comparison of performance with industry and world leaders

+ Strengths

1.

2.

3.

– Opportunities for improvement

1.

2.

3.

Strategic planning issues

Short-term (one to three years)

1.

2.

Long-term (three years or more)

1.

2.

6.4 Notes

6.4 Supplier Quality Results (35 points)

Summarize trends in quality and current quality levels of suppliers. Compare the organization's supplier quality with that of competitors and/or with appropriate benchmarks.

Areas to Address

a. Trends and current levels for key measures and/or indicators of supplier quality performance.

b. Comparison of the organization's supplier quality levels with those of appropriately selected companies and/or benchmarks.

[ ]   **6.4** PERCENT SCORE

[ ] Approach   [ ] Deployment   [✓] Results

6.4a   Does your organization track improvement of your key suppliers?

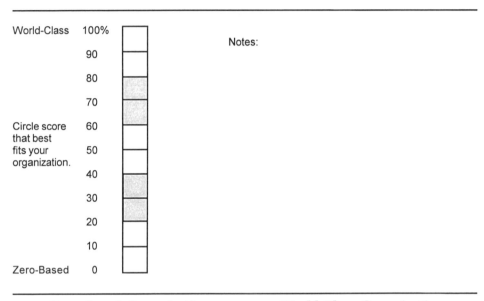

World-Class   100%
                90
                80
                70
Circle score   60
that best
fits your   50
organization.
                40
                30
                20
                10
Zero-Based   0

Notes:

Zero-Based Organization

- *Quality audits of suppliers are not performed.*

- *Organization does not have a vendor/supplier program plan.*

World-Class Organization

- *Quality audits of suppliers are performed.*

- *Organization tracks supplier performance.*

☐ Approach   ☐ Deployment   ☑ Results

6.4a   Supplier-quality results

+ Strengths

   1.

   2.

   3.

– Opportunities for improvement

   1.

   2.

   3.

Strategic planning issues

   Short-term (one to three years)

   1.

   2.

   Long-term (three years or more)

   1.

   2.

6.4b *How does your key suppliers' quality compare to that of industry competitors and/or to benchmark organizations?*

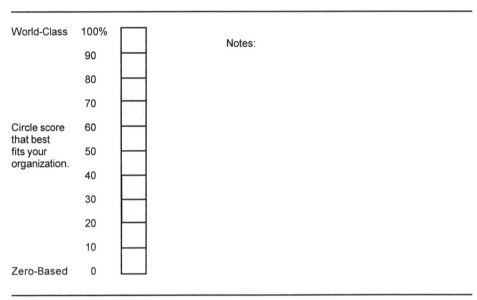

World-Class 100%

90

80

70

Circle score 60
that best
fits your 50
organization.
40

30

20

10

Zero-Based 0

Notes:

Zero-Based Organization

- *Organization has no understanding of benchmark process.*

- *No supplier quality comparisons are made by organization.*

World-Class Organization

- *Organization conducts supplier-quality benchmarks.*

- *Organization compares supplier-quality levels against industry and principal competitors' supplier-quality levels.*

☐ Approach ☐ Deployment ✓ Results

6.4b   Supplier comparisons with industry and world leaders

+ Strengths

  1.

  2.

  3.

– Opportunities for improvement

  1.

  2.

  3.

Strategic planning issues

  Short-term (one to three years)

  1.

  2.

  Long-term (three years or more)

  1.

  2.

Source of the following: 1994 Award Criteria;
Malcolm Baldrige National Quality Award examination
items and notes are excerpted throughout
Measuring Up to the Baldrige.

7.0

Customer Focus and Satisfaction

Total section value: 300 points

The *Customer Focus and Satisfaction* category examines the organization's relationship with customers and its knowledge of customer requirements and of the key quality factors that determine marketplace competitiveness. Also examined are the organization's methods to determine customer satisfaction, current needs and levels of satisfaction, and those results relative to competitors.

7.1 Notes

7.1 Customer Expectations: Current and Future (35 points)

Describe how the organization determines near-term and longer-term requirements and expectations of customers.

Areas to Address

a. How the organization determines *current and near-term requirements* and expectations of customers. Include (1) how customer groups and/or market segments are determined or selected, including how customers of competitors and other potential customers are considered; (2) how information is collected, including what information is sought, frequency and methods of collection, and how objectivity and validity are assured; (3) how specific product-and-service features and the relative importance of these features to customer groups or segments are determined; and (4) how other key information and data such as complaints, gains and losses of customers, and product/service performance are used to support the determination.

b. How the organization addresses *future requirements* and expectations of customers. Include (1) the time horizon for the determination; (2) how important technological, competitive, societal, environmental, economic, and demographic factors that may bear upon customer requirements, expectations, preferences, or alternatives are considered; (3) how customers of competitors and other potential customers are considered; (4) how key product-and-service features and the relative importance of these features are projected; and (5) how changing or emerging market segments and their implications on current or new product/service lines are considered.

c. How the organization evaluates and improves its processes for determining customer requirements and expectations.

☐ 7.1 PERCENT SCORE

☑ Approach ☑ Deployment ☐ Results

7.1a *How does your organization determine current and near-term requirements and expectations of customers (e.g., customer focus groups, third-party surveys, etc.)?*

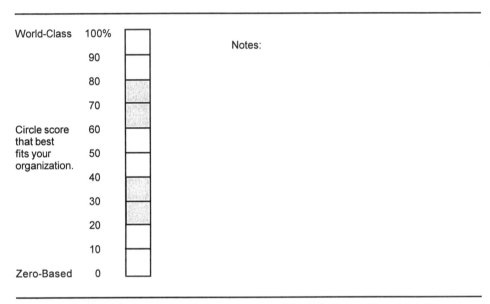

Zero-Based Organization

- No end-user surveys are conducted.

- Customers are not segmented and surveyed regarding their requirements and expectations.

World-Class Organization

- Current and near-term requirements and expectations are determined by surveys, focus groups, and benchmark data.

- Organization holds semi-annual customer focus groups and surveys to ensure customer expectations are being met.

✓ Approach   ✓ Deployment   ☐ Results

7.1a   *How organization addresses current and near-term requirements and expectations of customers*

+ Strengths

  1.

  2.

  3.

− Opportunities for improvement

  1.

  2.

  3.

Strategic planning issues

  Short-term (one to three years)

  1.

  2.

  Long-term (three years or more)

  1.

  2.

*7.1b   How does your organization determine future new product/service
         lines for customers?*

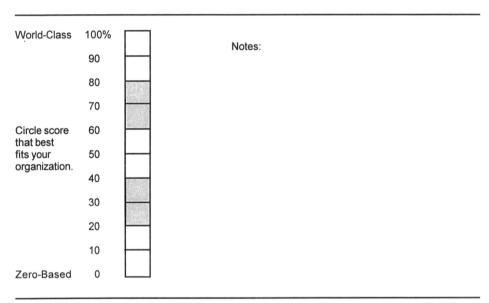

World-Class   100%

90

80

70

Circle score   60
that best
fits your   50
organization.
40

30

20

10

Zero-Based   0

Notes:

Zero-Based Organization	World-Class Organization
• *No competitive or industry benchmarking takes place to help determine future product/service features for customers.*	• *Cross-functional teams undertake task of projecting future requirements and expectations of customers.*
• *Organization does not address future requirements and expectations of customers.*	• *Customer-contact employees meet monthly to determine future customer requirements and expectations.*

☑ Approach   ☑ Deployment   ☐ Results

7.1b   Determining future product/service features

+ Strengths

   1.

   2.

   3.

– Opportunities for improvement

   1.

   2.

   3.

Strategic planning issues

   Short-term (one to three years)

     1.

     2.

   Long-term (three years or more)

     1.

     2.

7.1c   *How does your organization evaluate and improve its process for determining customer requirements and expectations?*

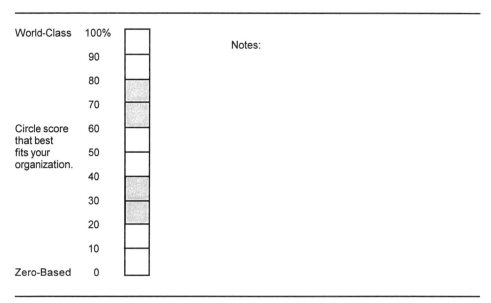

World-Class 100%	Notes:
90	
80	
70	
Circle score 60 that best	
fits your 50 organization.	
40	
30	
20	
10	
Zero-Based 0	

Zero-Based Organization	*World-Class Organization*
• *Organization appears weak in evaluating customer requirements and expectations.*	• *Organization uses customer focus groups and customer advisory council to address customer requirements and expectations.*
• *Organization does not have process in place to determine customer requirements and expectations.*	• *Organization has survey process in place to determine customer requirements and expectations.*

✓ Approach   ✓ Deployment   ☐ Results

7.1c   Evaluating and improving customer requirements and expectations

+ Strengths

   1.

   2.

   3.

– Opportunities for improvement

   1.

   2.

   3.

Strategic planning issues

   Short-term (one to three years)

   1.

   2.

   Long-term (three years or more)

   1.

   2.

7.2 Notes

7.2 Customer Relationship Management (65 points)

Describe how the organization provides effective management of its interactions and relationships with its customers, and how it uses information gained from customers to improve customer-relationship management processes.

Areas to Address

a. For the organization's most important contacts between its employees and customers, summarize the key requirements for maintaining and building relationships. Describe how these requirements are translated into key quality measures.

b. How service standards based upon the key quality measures (7.2a) are set and used. Include (1) how service standards, including measures and performance levels, are deployed to customer-contact employees and to other organizational units that provide support for customer-contact employees; and (2) how the performance of the overall service standards system is tracked.

c. How the organization provides information and easy access so as to enable customers to seek assistance, comment, and complain. Include the main types of contact and how easy access is maintained for each type.

d. How the organization follows up with customers on products, services, and recent transactions to seek feedback and to help build relationships.

e. How the organization ensures that formal and informal complaints and feedback received by all organizational units are resolved effectively and promptly. Briefly describe the complaint management process.

f. How the following are addressed for customer-contact employees: (1) selection factors; (2) career path; (3) deployment of special training to include knowledge of products and services, listening to customers, soliciting comments from customers, how to anticipate and handle problems or failures ("recovery"), skills in customer retention, and how to manage expectations; (4) empowerment and decision making; (5) satisfaction; and (6) recognition and reward.

g. How the organization evaluates and improves its customer-relationship management processes. Include (1) how the organization seeks opportunities to enhance relationships with all customers or with key customers; (2) how evaluations lead to improvement, such as in service standards, access, customer-contact employee training, and technology support; and (3) how customer information is used in the improvement process.

7.2 PERCENT SCORE

☑ Approach ☑ Deployment ☐ Results

7.2a   *How does your organization maintain and build customer*
         relationships?

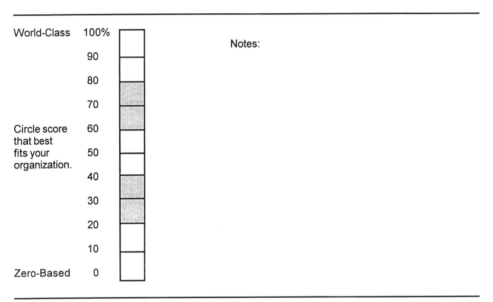

World-Class   100%

Notes:

              90

              80

              70

Circle score 60
that best
fits your   50
organization.
              40

              30

              20

              10

Zero-Based   0

Zero-Based Organization

- *No system, strategy, plan, or method exists to understand basic customer needs.*

- *Organization does not conduct exit interviews with customers.*

World-Class Organization

- *Customer advisory board in place.*

- *Round-table executive sessions held with customers.*

☑ Approach   ☑ Deployment   ☐ Results

7.2a   Organization's determination of most important factors in
*   maintaining and building customer relationships*

+ Strengths

   1.

   2.

   3.

− Opportunities for improvement

   1.

   2.

   3.

Strategic planning issues

   Short-term (one to three years)

   1.

   2.

   Long-term (three years or more)

   1.

   2.

7.2b   *What does your organization do to develop the service standards for customer-contact personnel?*

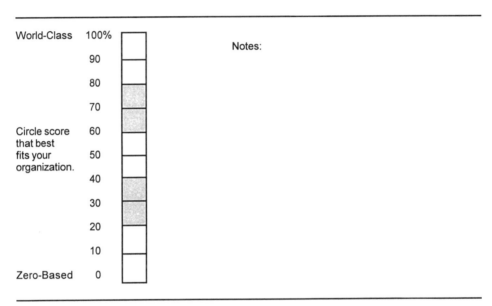

World-Class	100%
	90
	80
	70
Circle score that best fits your organization.	60
	50
	40
	30
	20
	10
Zero-Based	0

Notes:

Zero-Based Organization

- *No customer-contact training exists.*

- *Organization does not define service standards for customer-contact employees.*

World-Class Organization

- *Customer-contact personnel are taught state-of-the-art customer-service skills.*

- *Service standards that define reliability, responsiveness, and effectiveness are based on customer input and deployed to customer-contact personnel.*

✓ Approach   ✓ Deployment   ☐ Results

7.2b   *Customer-contact service standards set*

+ Strengths

   1.

   2.

   3.

– Opportunities for improvement

   1.

   2.

   3.

Strategic planning issues

   Short-term (one to three years)

   1.

   2.

   Long-term (three years or more)

   1.

   2.

7.2c   How does your organization ensure that customers can easily
        comment on your organization's products or services?

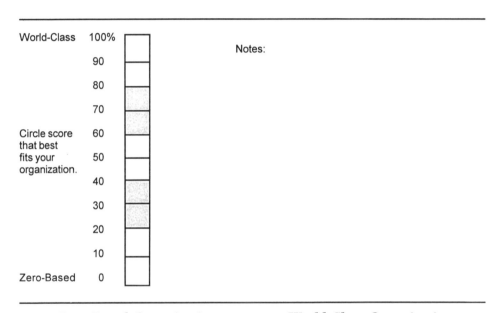

Zero-Based Organization	World-Class Organization
• Customer input is not encouraged.	• Customer focus groups in existence.
• Organization does not provide easy access for customers.	• An 800 number is installed for customer assistance.

☑ Approach   ☑ Deployment   ☐ Results

7.2c   Organization provides easy access for customer assistance

+ Strengths

1.

2.

3.

– Opportunities for improvement

1.

2.

3.

Strategic planning issues

Short-term (one to three years)

1.

2.

Long-term (three years or more)

1.

2.

7.2d   *How frequent, thorough, and objective is your organization's follow-up to customers on products, services, and recent transactions?*

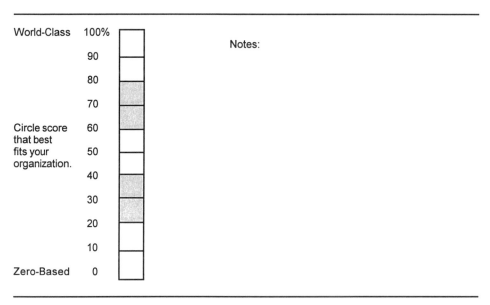

World-Class   100%

90

80

70

Circle score   60
that best
fits your   50
organization.

40

30

20

10

Zero-Based   0

Notes:

Zero-Based Organization	**World-Class Organization**
• *No customer follow-up process exists.*	• *Process methodologies developed to analyze customer complaints.*
• *Customer follow-up is not considered a priority by organization.*	• *Documented follow-up process for customers on products, services, and recent transactions in place.*

✓ Approach   ✓ Deployment   ☐ Results

7.2d Customer follow-up

+ Strengths

  1.

  2.

  3.

– Opportunities for improvement

  1.

  2.

  3.

Strategic planning issues

  Short-term (one to three years)

  1.

  2.

  Long-term (three years or more)

  1.

  2.

7.2e   How does your organization analyze and use customer complaints and feedback?

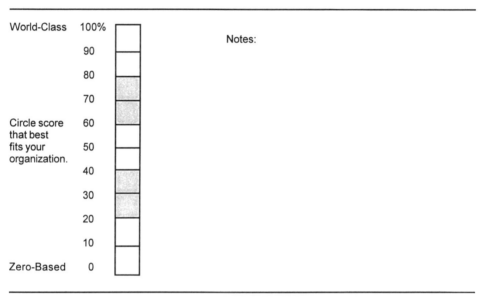

World-Class   100%

Notes:

90

80

70

Circle score   60
that best
fits your   50
organization.

40

30

20

10

Zero-Based   0

Zero-Based Organization

- *Organization does not collect formal and informal complaints from customers.*

- *Organization relies on customer-contact employees to manage customer complaints individually.*

World-Class Organization

- *Organization collects all formal and informal customer complaints and feedback and enters them into a data base in their mainframe computer. These data are then distributed to appropriate departments.*

- *Organization uses customer complaint data to improve customer-contact training.*

☑ Approach   ☑ Deployment   ☐ Results

7.2e   *Customer complaints aggregated for overall evaluation*

+ Strengths

    1.

    2.

    3.

– Opportunities for improvement

    1.

    2.

    3.

Strategic planning issues

    Short-term (one to three years)

    1.

    2.

    Long-term (three years or more)

    1.

    2.

7.2f   *How does your organization ensure that employees who have
        contact with customers are selected properly and given the latest,
        state-of-the-art tools and training that your organization can afford?*

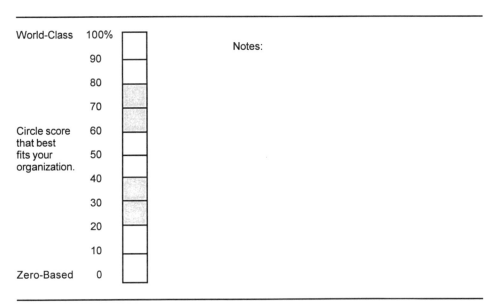

World-Class	100%
	90
	80
	70
Circle score that best fits your organization.	60
	50
	40
	30
	20
	10
Zero-Based	0

Notes:

Zero-Based Organization	*World-Class Organization*
• *Customer contact is neither rated nor rewarded within the organization.*	• *Customer contact is considered an integral part of the organization.*
• *No selection process is in place for customer-contact employees.*	• *Customer-contact employees are given recognition and rewards for improved customer service.*

☑ Approach   ☑ Deployment   ☐ Results

7.2f   Selection, training, and development of customer-contact employees

+ Strengths

    1.

    2.

    3.

– Opportunities for improvement

    1.

    2.

    3.

Strategic planning issues

    Short-term (one to three years)

    1.

    2.

    Long-term (three years or more)

    1.

    2.

7.2g   *How does your organization evaluate its performance in managing relationships with customers?*

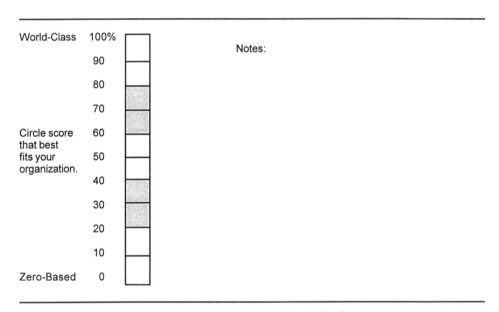

Notes:

Zero-Based Organization	World-Class Organization
• No formal process exists for improving customer relationships.	• Formal process in place to improve relationships with customers (e.g., customer service training, published customer service standards, etc.).
• Customer-relationship evaluation and training does not exist within the organization.	• All customer information is used to improve customer-relationship

☑ Approach   ☑ Deployment   ☐ Results

7.2g   Organization's customer-relationship management practices

+ Strengths

   1.

   2.

   3.

– Opportunities for improvement

   1.

   2.

   3.

Strategic planning issues

   Short-term (one to three years)

   1.

   2.

   Long-term (three years or more)

   1.

   2.

7.3 Notes

7.3 Commitment to Customers (15 points)

Describe the organization's commitments to customers regarding its products/services and how these commitments are evaluated and improved.

Areas to Address

a. Types of commitments the organization makes to promote trust and confidence in its products/services and to satisfy customers when product/service failures occur. Describe these commitments and how they (1) address the principal concerns of customers, (2) are free from conditions that might weaken customers' trust and confidence, and (3) are communicated to customers clearly and simply.

b. How the organization evaluates and improves its commitments, and the customers' understanding of them, to avoid gaps between customer expectations and organization performance. Include (1) how information/feedback from customers is used, (2) how product/service performance improvement data are used, and (3) how competitors' commitments are considered.

7.3
PERCENT
SCORE

☑ Approach   ☑ Deployment   ☐ Results

7.3a   *How does your organization promote trust and confidence in its products, services, and relationships? (For example, does it offer a written warranty, or a simple understanding of its guarantee?)*

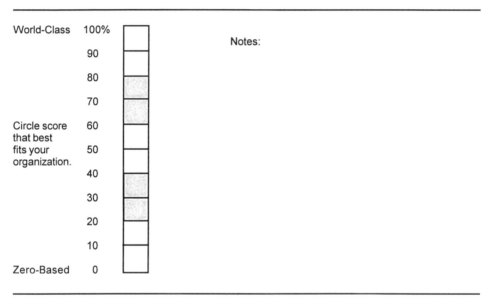

World-Class   100%

                90   Notes:

                80

                70

Circle score   60
that best
fits your   50
organization.
                40

                30

                20

                10

Zero-Based   0

Zero-Based Organization	*World-Class Organization*

- *No written warranties/guaran-tees for products/services issued.*

- *Guarantees are written in language that is hard for customers to understand.*

- *Organization issues written war-ranty/guarantee for all products/ services in understandable language.*

- *Installation of toll-free numbers for customer responses.*

☑ Approach   ☑ Deployment   ☐ Results

7.3a   Organization's commitments to promote trust and confidence in its products, services, and relationships

+ Strengths

   1.

   2.

   3.

– Opportunities for improvement

   1.

   2.

   3.

Strategic planning issues

   Short-term (one to three years)

   1.

   2.

   Long-term (three years or more)

   1.

   2.

7.3b   *How does your organization evaluate and improve your customers'*
understanding of your commitments?

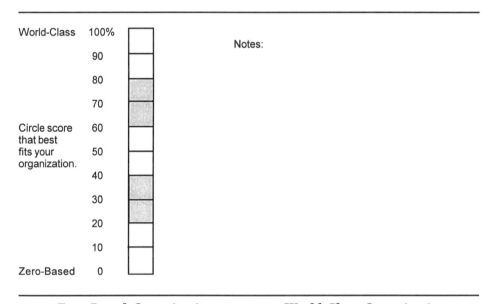

Zero-Based Organization	World-Class Organization
• *No customer survey conducted to gauge customer understanding of commitments.*	• *Organization conducts surveys and customer focus meetings (formal and informal) to continuously improve its commitments.*
• *Feedback from customers is not used to gauge customer understanding of organization's commitments.*	• *All product-and-service warranties are written in simple, understandable language.*

☑ Approach   ☑ Deployment   ☑ Results

7.3b   *Evaluating and improving understanding of organization's customer commitments*

+ Strengths

   1.

   2.

   3.

– Opportunities for improvement

   1.

   2.

   3.

Strategic planning issues

   Short-term (one to three years)

   1.

   2.

   Long-term (three years or more)

   1.

   2.

7.4 Notes

7.4 Customer Satisfaction Determination (30 points)

Describe how the organization determines customer satisfaction, customer repurchase intentions, and customer satisfaction relative to competitors.

Describe how these determination processes are evaluated and improved.

Areas to Address

a. How the organization determines customer satisfaction. Include (1) a brief description of processes and measurement scales used, frequency of determination, and how objectivity and validity are assured. Indicate significant differences, if any, in processes and measurement scales for different customer groups or segments; and (2) how customer satisfaction measurements capture key information that reflects customers' likely future market behavior, such as repurchase intentions or positive referrals.

b. How customer satisfaction relative to that for competitors is determined. Describe (1) organization-based comparative studies and (2) comparative studies or evaluations made by independent organizations and/or customers. For (1) and (2), describe how objectivity and validity of studies are ensured.

c. How the organization evaluates and improves its overall processes and measurement scales for determining customer satisfaction and customer satisfaction relative to that for competitors. Include how other indicators (such as gains and losses of customers) and customer dissatisfaction indicators (such as complaints) are used in this improvement process.

☐ 7.4
PERCENT
SCORE

☑ Approach   ☑ Deployment   ☐ Results

265

7.4a   How does your organization determine customer satisfaction for its different customer groups?

World-Class   100%

90

80

70

Circle score   60
that best
fits your   50
organization.

40

30

20

10

Zero-Based   0

Notes:

Zero-Based Organization

- *No evidence that management regularly reviews customer satisfaction trends and indicators and does not take deliberate actions to change processes to improve customer satisfaction.*

- *Organization does not recognize differences in customers.*

World-Class Organization

- *Organization determines customer satisfaction for its different customer groups through its annual customer survey.*

- *Customer focus groups are divided up among different customer groups.*

☑ Approach   ☑ Deployment   ☐ Results

7.4a   *Organization's determination of customer satisfaction for different customer groups*

+ Strengths

1.

2.

3.

– Opportunities for improvement

1.

2.

3.

Strategic planning issues

Short-term (one to three years)

1.

2.

Long-term (three years or more)

1.

2.

7.4b   *How does your organization's customer satisfaction level compare to that of your competitors?*

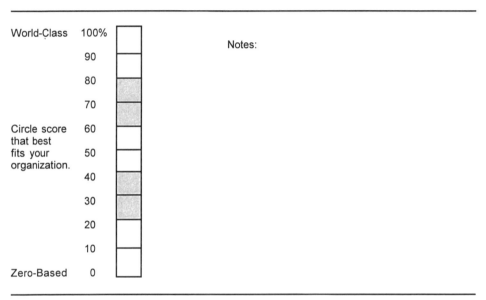

Zero-Based Organization	World-Class Organization
• No data exist to determine customer satisfaction.	• Customer surveys and customer focus groups are used to collect data regarding competitors.
• Organization has no concern for comparing its customers' satisfaction against competitors.	• Employees are encouraged to visit and benchmark competitors.

☑ Approach   ☑ Deployment   ☐ Results

7.4b   Organization's determination of customer satisfaction relative to competitors

+ Strengths

   1.

   2.

   3.

– Opportunities for improvement

   1.

   2.

   3.

Strategic planning issues

   Short-term (one to three years)

   1.

   2.

   Long-term (three years or more)

   1.

   2.

7.4c   *How does your organization evaluate and improve its approach to*
        determining customer satisfaction relative to that of competitors?

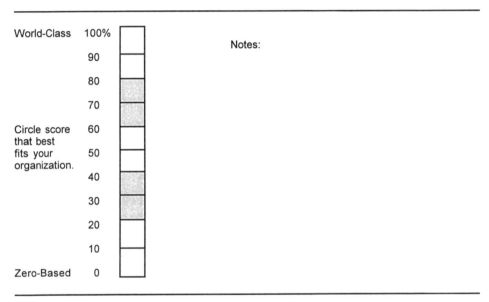

World-Class   100%

              90

              80

              70

Circle score 60
that best
fits your   50
organization.
              40

              30

              20

              10

Zero-Based   0

Notes:

Zero-Based Organization

- *No evidence that evaluation of customer satisfaction process is compared to competitors and industry leaders.*

- *Organization has no concern for how competitors determine customer satisfaction.*

World-Class Organization

- *Organization involves customer-contact employees in determining customer satisfaction relative to that of competitors.*

- *Competitor focus groups are conducted to help determine organization's customer satisfaction relative to that for competitors.*

☑ Approach   ☑ Deployment   ☐ Results

7.4c   *Evaluation and improvement methods used for determining*
        customer satisfaction relative to that of competitors

+ Strengths

  1.

  2.

  3.

− Opportunities for improvement

  1.

  2.

  3.

Strategic planning issues

  Short-term (one to three years)

  1.

  2.

  Long-term (three years or more)

  1.

  2.

7.5 Notes

7.5 Customer Satisfaction Results (85 points)

Summarize trends in the organization's customer satisfaction and trends in key indicators of customer dissatisfaction.

Areas to Address

a. Trends and current levels in key measures and/or indicators of customer satisfaction, including customer retention. Segment by customer group, as appropriate. Trends may be supported by objective information and/or data from customers demonstrating current or recent (past three years) satisfaction with the organization's products/services.

b. Trends in measures and/or indicators of customer dissatisfaction. Address the most relevant and important indicators for the organization's products/services.

7.5
PERCENT
SCORE

☑ Approach ☑ Deployment ☐ Results

7.5a   *Do you collect trend data that measure customer satisfaction and customer retention?*

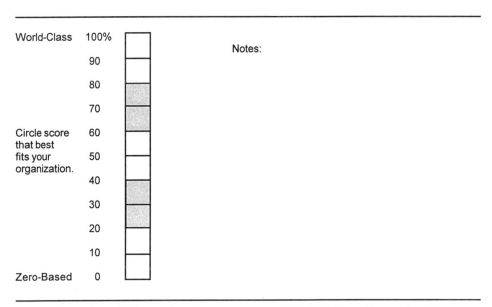

Notes:

Zero-Based Organization	World-Class Organization
• No data available to determine trends.	• Organization segments trend data by customer groups.
• Organization does not use trend data to determine customer satisfaction and customer retention.	• Organization uses customer trend data in its planning process.

☑ Approach   ☑ Deployment   ☐ Results

7.5a   Trend data on customer satisfaction and customer retention

+ Strengths

 1.

 2.

 3.

– Opportunities for improvement

 1.

 2.

 3.

Strategic planning issues

 Short-term (one to three years)

 1.

 2.

 Long-term (three years or more)

 1.

 2.

7.5b *Does your organization measure adverse customer indicators, such as complaints, claims, refunds, no call returns, repeat services, litigation, replacements, downgrades, warranty costs, and warranty work?*

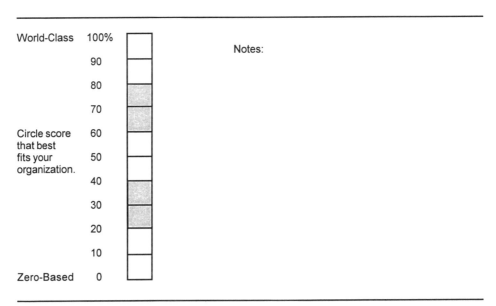

Notes:

Zero-Based Organization	World-Class Organization
• *No documented follow-up methods, disciplines, controls, and processes in place to address adverse customer indicators.*	• *Organization leads competitors and industry leaders in reducing adverse customer indicators.*
• *Customer dissatisfaction is not addressed.*	• *Adverse customer indicators are shared with all customer-contact employees.*

☐ Approach   ☐ Deployment   ☑ Results

7.5b   Trend data on customer dissatisfaction

+ Strengths

   1.

   2.

   3.

– Opportunities for improvement

   1.

   2.

   3.

Strategic planning issues

   Short-term (one to three years)

     1.

     2.

   Long-term (three years or more)

     1.

     2.

7.6 Notes

7.6 Customer Satisfaction Comparison (70 points)

Compare the organization's customer satisfaction results with those of competitors.

Areas to Address

a. Trends and current levels in key measures and/or indicators of customer satisfaction relative to competitors. Segment by customer group, as appropriate. Trends may be supported by objective information and/or data from independent organizations, including customers.

b. Trends in gaining and losing customers, or customer accounts, to competitors.

c. Trends in gaining or losing market share to competitors.

| | 7.6 PERCENT SCORE |

☐ Approach ☐ Deployment ☑ Results

279

7.6a   Does your organization collect data that measure customer satisfaction with your products and/or services against satisfaction with competitors' products/services?

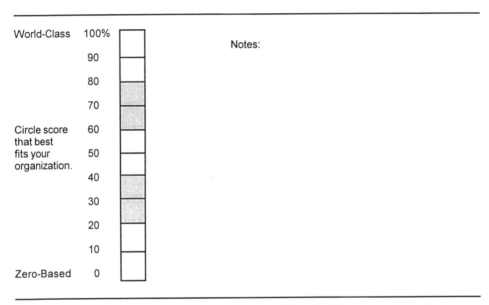

World-Class   100%

90

80

70

Circle score   60
that best
fits your   50
organization.

40

30

20

10

Zero-Based   0

Notes:

Zero-Based Organization

- Organization does not collect customer satisfaction data relative to its competition.

- Organization is not concerned with measuring customer satisfaction relative to competitors.

World-Class Organization

- Competitive comparisons show positive trends.

- Relative to competition, organization shows positive trend.

☐ Approach   ☐ Deployment   ☑ Results

7.6a   Comparative trends of customer satisfaction relative to competitors

+ Strengths

   1.

   2.

   3.

– Opportunities for improvement

   1.

   2.

   3.

Strategic planning issues

   Short-term (one to three years)

   1.

   2.

   Long-term (three years or more)

   1.

   2.

7.6b   Does your organization measure customer turnover?

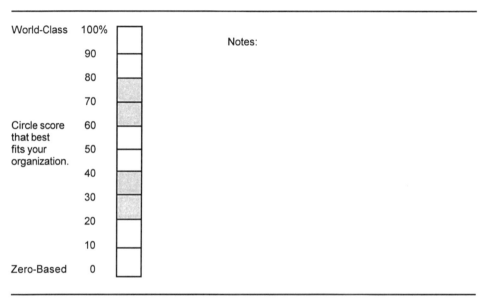

World-Class   100%

90

80

70

Circle score   60
that best
fits your   50
organization.

40

30

20

10

Zero-Based   0

Notes:

Zero-Based Organization	*World-Class Organization*
• *Organization does not measure customer turnover.*	• *Customer turnover is measured.*
	• *Customer exit interviews conducted.*
• *No trend data are accumulated on customer loss to competitors.*	

☐ Approach   ☐ Deployment   ☑ Results

7.6b   *Trends in gaining or losing customers to competitors*

+ Strengths

  1.

  2.

  3.

– Opportunities for improvement

  1.

  2.

  3.

Strategic planning issues

  Short-term (one to three years)

  1.

  2.

  Long-term (three years or more)

  1.

  2.

7.6c   *Do trends indicate that your organization's market share has increased as a result of its quality-improvement efforts?*

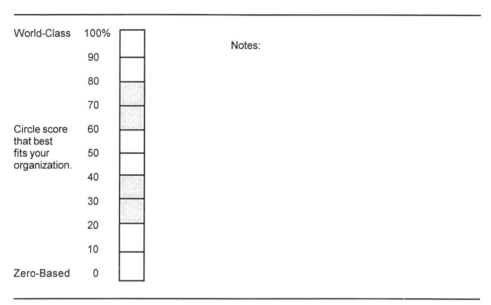

World-Class   100%

Notes:

90

80

70

Circle score   60
that best
fits your   50
organization.

40

30

20

10

Zero-Based   0

Zero-Based Organization	*World-Class Organization*

- *Organization is weak in measuring market share against major competitors.*

- *Organization does not use trend data to determine gains or losses of market share to competitors.*

- *Market share has increased 10 percent or more over the past three years as a result of organization's customer focus.*

- *Organization uses trend analysis to gauge market share improvement.*

☐ Approach   ☐ Deployment   ☑ Results

7.6c   *Trends in gaining or losing market share relative to major competitors*

+ Strengths

1.

2.

3.

– Opportunities for improvement

1.

2.

3.

Strategic planning issues

Short-term (one to three years)

1.

2.

Long-term (three years or more)

1.

2.

Summary of Assessment Items Score Sheet

		Total Points Possible A	Percent Score 0–100% (10% units) B	Score (A x B) C
1.0	**Leadership**			
1.1	Senior executive leadership . . .	45	_____ %	_____
1.2	Management for quality	25	_____ %	_____
1.3	Public responsibility and corporate citizenship	25	_____ %	_____
	CATEGORY TOTAL	**95**		_____ (Sum C)
2.0	**Information and Analysis**			
2.1	Scope and management of quality and performance data and information	15	_____ %	_____
2.2	Competitive comparisons and benchmarking	20	_____ %	_____
2.3	Analysis and uses of organization-level data	40	_____ %	_____
	CATEGORY TOTAL	**75**		_____ (Sum C)
3.0	**Strategic Quality Planning**			
3.1	Strategic quality and organization performance planning process.	35	_____ %	_____
3.2	Quality and performance plans	25	_____ %	_____
	CATEGORY TOTAL	**60**		_____ (Sum C)

		Total Points Possible	Percent Score 0–100% (10% units)	Score (A x B)
		A	B	C

4.0 Human Resources Development and Management

4.1	Human resources development and management	20	_____%	_____
4.2	Employee involvement	40	_____%	_____
4.3	Employee education and training	40	_____%	_____
4.4	Employee performance and recognition	25	_____%	_____
4.5	Employee well-being and satisfaction.	25	_____%	_____
	CATEGORY TOTAL	**150**		_____ (Sum C)

5.0 Management of Process Quality

5.1	Design and introduction of quality products and services. .	40	_____%	_____
5.2	Process management: product and service production and delivery processes	35	_____%	_____
5.3	Process management: business processes and support service .	30	_____%	_____
5.4	Supplier quality.	20	_____%	_____
5.5	Quality assessment	15	_____%	_____
	CATEGORY TOTAL	**140**		_____ (Sum C)

6.0 Quality and Operational Results

6.1	Product and service quality results	70	_____%	_____
6.2	Company operational results	50	_____%	_____
6.3	Business and support service results	25	_____%	_____
6.4	Supplier quality results	35	_____%	_____
	CATEGORY TOTAL	**180**		_____ (Sum C)

			Total Points Possible	Percent Score 0–100% (10% units)	Score (A x B)
			A	B	C

7.0   Customer Focus and Satisfaction

7.1	Customer expectations: current and future	35		_____ %	_____
7.2	Customer relationship management	65		_____ %	_____
7.3	Commitment to customers.	15		_____ %	_____
7.4	Customer satisfaction determination	30		_____ %	_____
7.5	Customer satisfaction results	85		_____ %	_____
7.6	Customer satisfaction comparison	70		_____ %	_____
	CATEGORY TOTAL	**300**			_____
				(Sum C)	

TOTAL POINTS   **1000**   _____

APPENDIXES

Appendix A

Baldrige Readiness Assessment Bar Graph

Bar graphs display opportunities for improvement.

Users can shade in assessment percentages on bar graphs from item score boxes located throughout this manual.

1.0 Leadership

World-Class 100%
80
60
40
20
Zero-Based 0

Items | 1.1 | 1.2 | 1.3

1.1	Senior executive leadership
1.2	Management for quality
1.3	Public responsibility and corporate citizenship

2.0 Information & Analysis

World-Class 100%
80
60
40
20
Zero-Based 0

Items | 2.1 | 2.2 | 2.3

2.1	Scope and management of quality and performance data and information
2.2	Competitive comparisons and benchmarking
2.3	Analysis and uses of organization-level data

Note: Based on bar graphs, select item(s) that have lowest score and prioritize strategic opportunities for improvement.

Leadership improvement prioritites

Priority 1 _____

_____

Priority 2 _____

_____

Priority 3 _____

_____

Information and analysis improvement priorities

Priority 1 _____

_____

Priority 2 _____

_____

Priority 3 _____

_____

3.0 Strategic Quality Planning

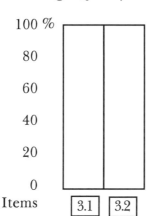

Items   3.1   3.2

3.1 Strategic quality and
    organizational performance
    planning process

3.2 Quality and performance
    plans

4.0 Human Resource Development
     and Management

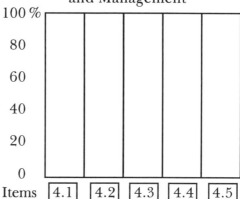

Items   4.1   4.2   4.3   4.4   4.5

4.1 Human resource planning and
    management
4.2 Employee involvement

4.3 Employee education and
    training
4.4 Employee performance and
    recognition
4.5 Employee well-being and
    satisfaction

Note: Based on bar graphs, select item(s) that have lowest score and prioritize strategic opportunities for improvement.

Strategic quality planning
improvement priorities

Priority 1 _____
_____

Priority 2 _____
_____

Priority 3 _____
_____

Human resources development
and management improvement
priorities

Priority 1 _____
_____

Priority 2 _____
_____

Priority 3 _____
_____

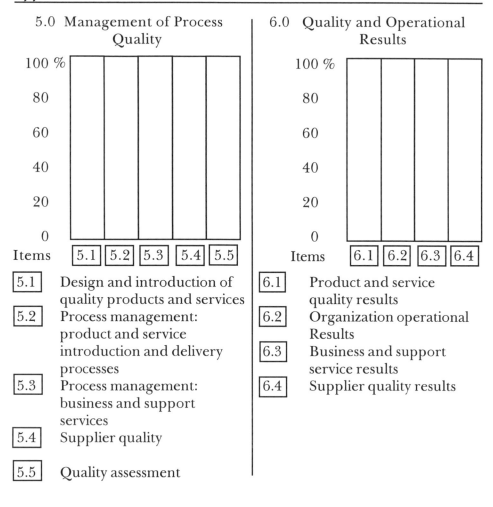

5.0 Management of Process Quality

| Items | 5.1 | 5.2 | 5.3 | 5.4 | 5.5 |

5.1 Design and introduction of quality products and services
5.2 Process management: product and service introduction and delivery processes
5.3 Process management: business and support services
5.4 Supplier quality
5.5 Quality assessment

6.0 Quality and Operational Results

| Items | 6.1 | 6.2 | 6.3 | 6.4 |

6.1 Product and service quality results
6.2 Organization operational Results
6.3 Business and support service results
6.4 Supplier quality results

Note: Based on bar graphs, select item(s) that have lowest score and prioritize strategic opportunities for improvement.

Management of process quality improvement priorities

Priority 1 _____

Priority 2 _____

Priority 3 _____

Quality and operational results improvement priorities

Priority 1 _____

Priority 2 _____

Priority 3 _____

7.0 Customer Focus and Satisfaction

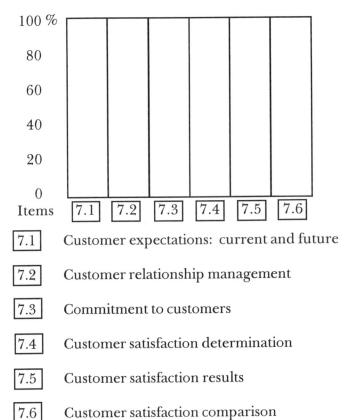

Items	7.1	Customer expectations: current and future
	7.2	Customer relationship management
	7.3	Commitment to customers
	7.4	Customer satisfaction determination
	7.5	Customer satisfaction results
	7.6	Customer satisfaction comparison

Note: Based on bar graphs, select item(s) that have lowest score and prioritize strategic opportunities for improvement.

Customer focus and satisfaction
improvement priorities

Priority 1 _____

_____

Priority 2 _____

_____

Priority 3 _____

_____

Appendix B

Malcolm Baldrige National Quality Award Written Application Checklist

This detailed checklist will aid your organization in preparing a written application for a quality award that is based on Baldrige criteria.

_____ 1. Cite competitive benchmarking trips.

_____ 2. Document positive trend analyses charted.

_____ 3. Cite examples of satisfying customers beyond expectations.

_____ 4. Document all customer-satisfaction awards over past several years.

_____ 5. Document organization's involvement with customer teams.

_____ 6. Document companies that benchmarked your organization; include letters or any correspondence received from customers.

_____ 7. Retain in your files any control charts that show trends, either negative or positive, and document what your organization did to improve negative trends.

_____ 8. Insert information about your organization's corporate vision (values) statement and how it drives relationships with customers, employees, and suppliers.

_____ 9. Document speeches given by senior officers regarding quality improvement within community/industry.

_____ 10. Document all speeches given at every employee level that refer to quality improvement within your organization.

_____ 11. Document written endorsements from major customers about quality of your products/services, etc.

_____ 12. Solicit letters from governor or mayor acknowledging your organization's total quality initiatives.

_____ 13. Solicit letters from senior management of supplier companies that supply your organization, regarding supplier partnership and certification issues.

_____ 14. Document literacy or other support programs that help employees maintain their quality of work life.

_____ 15. Document all customer surveys (internal and third-party).

_____ 16. Document customer satisfaction letters (e.g., product and process quality).

_____ 17. Document short-term (one to three years) and long-term (three years or more) strategic quality plans.

_____ 18. Document your organization's integration of its quality plan into the business plan.

_____ 19. Document employee suggestion-idea system (how many employees use the system).

_____ 20. Document employee recognition (be specific when explaining how you use this to drive improvement).

_____ 21. Document quality language used in your organization's employee newsletters and videos (produce a glossary of quality terms for employees).

_____ 22. Document supplier involvement, how your organization partners with suppliers and how suppliers' performance is measured.

_____ 23. Document any quality award initiatives—statewide, local, community, industry, or national—driven by the organization.

All data documented above should have a schedule to ensure completion.

Person responsible for collecting data _____

Date assignment is due _____ Date received _____

Appendix C

How to Order Copies
of the Award Material

The *Award Criteria* and the *Application Forms and Instructions* are
two separate documents.

Individual Orders:

Individual copies of either document can be obtained free of charge
from:

> Malcolm Baldrige National Quality Award
> National Institute of Standards and Technology
> Route 270 and Quince Orchard Road
> Administration Building, Room A537
> Gaithersburg, MD 20899-0001
> Telephone: 301-975-2036
> Telefax: 301-948-3716

Baldrige
Quick-Reference
Assessment Glossary

aggregated data   Data that an organization has gathered together into a mass or sum so as to constitute a whole. Aggregated data is collected and used to determine an organization's achievement levels and improvement trends.

Baldrige assessment   An organizational evaluation based on the seven categories, twenty-eight items, and ninety-one areas of the Malcolm Baldrige National Quality Award criteria.

benchmarking   A method whereby teams of employees review and visit best-in-class products, services, and practices. Benchmarking can include site visits to organizations and telephone interviews. Benchmarking is an involved process that organizations pursue when seeking to become world-class in processes that they have identified as needing improvement.

business processes and support services   Includes units and operations involving finance and accounting, software services, sales, marketing, public relations, information services, purchasing and personnel.

business ethics   A published statement of values and business ethics that are promoted and practiced both internally and externally by the organization.

business plan   A strategic plan that is published and shared throughout the organization. Many organizations that are beginning their quality improvement process have separate business plans and quality plans.

competitive comparisons   Comparisons of an organization's products/services against major competitors and industries.

control chart   A graph that is used by employees to determine if their work process is within prescribed limits.

cross-functional teams   Teams formed from different divisions or departments to solve or create new solutions to an organizational problem or opportunity.

customer   The end user of all products and services produced within an organization. Customers are both internal and external.

customer-contact employee   An employee who directly interfaces with external customers, in person, via telephone, or other means.

customer-relationship management   An organization's interactions and relationships with its customers.

cycle-time   The amount of time it takes to complete a specified work process.

data   The collection of facts, information, or statistics.

data analysis   The study, interpretation, and breakdown of data to help the organization gauge improvement.

documented improvement   A process improvement that has been supported against base-line data and documented at measured intervals.

ergonomics   The evaluation of an organization's facilities and equipment to ensure compatibility between workers and their work processes.

employee involvement   Involvement of employees across the organization at all levels.

employee morale   The attitudes of employees in regard to their willingness to perform work tasks.

empowerment   Employees' freedom to respond to customer demands and requests.

flowchart   A graphic map of a work process used by employee teams to document the current condition of a process.

goals and strategies   Organizations develop goals and strategies for short-term (one to three years) and long-term (three years or more) desired results. Goals and strategies are usually written and distributed across the organization.

improvement plan   A written plan that the organization has published to accomplish desired improvement results.

internal customer/supplier network   An organization's employee network, referred to as inside customers and suppliers.

key indicators   Key measures of performance (e.g., productivity, cycle time, cost, and other measures of effectiveness).

manufacturing organization   An organization that makes or processes raw materials into a finished product.

measurement   The process of gauging an organization's results against its customers' requirements.

mission statement   Many organizations have a published document that defines the organization's reason for existing. The mission statement is shared with employees, suppliers, and customers.

performance data   Results of improvements in product-and-service production and delivery processes.

process   A series of steps linked together to provide a product or service for an end user.

process control   A control device to detect and remove causes of variation in a defined process.

process management   An organization's maintenance of defined processes to ensure that both quality and performance are continuously improved.

productivity improvement   Measured reduction in an organization's key operational processes.

problem-solving tools   Tools used by teams to solve process problems (e.g., flowcharts, Pareto analysis, histograms, control charts, cause-and-effect diagrams, and matrix diagrams).

problem-solving teams   Cross-functional, work-group, departmental, or project focused teams that assess and analyze problems and are empowered by management to solve them.

public responsibility   Relates to an organization's possible impact on society with its products, services, and operations. Impact includes business ethics, environment, education, health care, community services, and safety effects as they relate to the public. Practices of trade or business associations are also considered part of an organization's public responsibility.

quality assessment   An assessment of an organization's approach to and implementation of quality.

quality plan   An organization that has just begun the quality-improvement process has a written quality plan. This plan is usually separate from the business plan. Organizations that are more mature in quality usually integrate their quality plan with their business plan.

quality results   An organization's achievement levels and improvement trends.

quality values   The standards, beliefs, and guiding principles by which an organization operates. These values are reflected in the way employees, suppliers, and customers are treated.

safe work practices   Organizations promote safety on the work site for employees. Many organizations have documented guidelines for employees to follow, and they collect data on safe work practices.

strategic plan   A detailed plan of action that an organization develops by establishing and defining measurable goals to achieve continuous quality improvement within an organization. A strategic plan can be broken into short-term (one to three years) and long-term (three years or more) components.

survey process   An organization's survey process can include customer surveys and employee surveys. Both survey processes help an organization to focus on internal/external customer satisfaction issues.

senior executive   Refers to the organization's highest-ranking official and those reporting directly to that official.

service organization   Nonmanufacturing organizations, such as utilities, schools, governments, transportation, finance, real estate, restaurants, hotels, news media, business services, professional services, and repair services.

small business   Complete businesses with not more than 500 full-time employees. Business activities may engage in manufacturing and/or service.

statistical process control (SPC)   Technique for measuring and analyzing process variations.

supplier   An individual or group, either internal to the organization or external, that provides input to a work-group or customer.

supplier certification program   A formal supplier program that an organizatiion uses to help improve supplier quality. Many organizations partner with critical suppliers and establish a relationship of trust and measurable results.

supplier partnership   A supplier process practiced by many organizations in both service and manufacturing. Organizations establish a preferred supplier program that is based on a trust relationship with measurable results. Supplier partnerships are usually a prelude to a more formalized supplier-certification program.

targets   Desired goals that organizations have in their strategic planning process.

third-party survey   A customer or employee survey conducted for the organization by a resource outside the organization.

total quality management (TQM)   A management philosophy that focuses on the internal/external customer throughout the organization.

user-friendly   A process that is understandable to employees.

values statement   Many organizations have a published document that describes their corporate beliefs. This values statement is usually shared with employees, suppliers, and customers.

vision statement   Many organizations have a published document that defines the corporate direction for the next five to ten years. The vision statement is shared with employees, suppliers, and customers.

world-class organization   An organization that produces excellent results in major areas with a sound quality management approach. This organization is totally integrated with a systematic, prevention-based system that is continuously refined through evaluations and improvement cycles.

zero-based organization   An organization that has no quality system in place. Its approach to quality management may, at best, be sound, systematic, effective, fully integrated, and implemented across the organization, but anecdotal in implementation.

Index